Town and Roof Gardens

Town and Roof Gardens

XENIA FIELD

Collins

St James's Place, London

1967

Printed in Great Britain
Collins Clear-Type Press
London and Glasgow

Contents

CONTENTS

Illustrations

Author's Note

My thanks are especially due to Mr H. Taylor, N.D.H., for his help and advice and for reading the proofs. Also to Mr A. Barber of Dobie's of Chester, Mr A. Bloom of Bressingham Nurseries, Mr H. S. J. Crane and Mr J. A. Dyter of Notcutt's, Mr S. M. Gault, Superintendent of Regent's Park, Mr F. A. Robinson of Greencourt Nurseries, Mr L. Russell of Sunningdale Nurseries, and to Landscape Architects Miss Sylvia Crowe and Mr du Gard Pasley and Landscape Designer Mr J. Brookes. Also to Redland Holdings for a brick design, photographers Mr H. Smith and Mr Ian Harris, and especially to Mr L. Turner, Secretary of the Royal National Rose Society. This list would not be complete without the name of my secretary, Mrs Dorothy Hobden.

The following have kindly allowed me to use photographs of their gardens in this book: Miss Bridget Boland, p. 97; Mr John Brookes, p. 144; Marchesa Carla Crosa, p. 160; Lady Macnaghten, p. 113; Mr Robert Stent, p. 112.

Introduction

In this country we excel in the art of gardening. Strangely, it is often only with middle-age that the taste shows itself and then only when we have a garden of our own and can experience the pleasures and pains of working among growing plants. After all, being ordered about in other people's gardens is something quite different and satisfies few. It is ownership and anticipation that makes the garden a perpetual delight—and the owner daily more proud.

I would call town gardening a challenge if I did not so dislike the word. However, in spite of the many difficulties that have to be overcome, there is today an unprecedented interest in growing flowers in built-up areas.

Enthusiasm among town gardeners has led to the transformation of backyards into patios and inner courts open to the sky—while roof gardens spring up in the night among the chimney-pots.

This is an ancient trend—from time immemorial, gardens have been outdoor rooms to many; arbours and shelters of fruit trees, vines or even bulrushes, have been tended by plant lovers.

The modern town garden should be closely associated with the house, so that finally it becomes almost part of it.

I Soil

London soil is dirty soil, and much the same can be said of any industrial town soil.

The top inch or two are polluted by fog, smoke and fumes and can be seen and felt to be soot-laden and grimy. Such soil is often impoverished if not altogether depleted of nourishment. It presents a problem.

The nurseryman would quite wisely suggest removing the two, three or more feet of tired soil and replacing it with a country loam. This is an ideal programme but an expensive one. Happily there is quite a good and far cheaper way out to suit all pockets.

Let the gardener aim at improving the top twelve inches of the soil, for it is within these inches that most plants feed. Then he must spot or specially feed trees and shrubs that have deeper-searching roots.

In my Holland Park garden where I worked for seven years I set out to feed the top twelve inches of the soil with humus. A load of farmyard manure from the country was a very handsome Christmas present, giving food, bulk and vitality to all who tasted it. And the joy about humus (and the Adam in us rejoices when it is well-rotted) is that it breaks up the heavy or enriches the light. But alas, it is not easy to come by and hop-manure, peat, garden loam or possibly a fertilizer has to be accepted in its place.

Fertilizers

The crusade against chemical fertilizers rages on, largely supported by countrymen who do not have to carry the 'muck' through the drawing-room. The townsman would be wise to keep out of the manure versus chemical ding-dong—and use both with discretion.

13

Organic fertilizers such as fish manure, hoof and horn meal, bonemeal and dried blood are safe and excellent, while any reputable general fertilizer acts as a chemical pep-up tonic. I have a liking for the general fertilizer of any reputable make. The fussy gardener collects special property-giving fertilizer packets by the dozen, as some women collect lipsticks; but as it is impossible to please every plant with any one product, it seems wisdom to offer a general one that will more or less suit all comers.

Chemical products are specifically and carefully balanced by the manufacturer and should be used strictly according to the given instructions. It is queer, but even mean men are apt to over-fertilize.

Lime

The modern gardener is bedevilled by the half-baked information so freely served up—on this occasion on the subject of lime-content in the soil. Is he, he anxiously enquires, acid or alkaline?

Well, if the test registers above pH7, the soil is alkaline and woe unto the gardener who tries to grow a rhododendron. ('A rhododendron set in lime looks like a curate doing time.'—Reginald Arkell.) If the test registers below pH7, then the soil is acid and the Rhododendron, Azalea, Camellia and the peat-lovers will thrive— but the Lilacs, Aquilegias, Carnations and Pinks will suffer.

There are numerous cheap soil-testing sets on the market, but should your soil fail to give satisfactory results after reasonable care and treatment, then it would be advisable to send a small sample from different parts of the garden to a horticultural research station for a professional report on the soil's condition and deficiencies. Levington Research Station (Fison's), Nr Ipswich, Suffolk, gives this helpful service free of charge.

Hydrated lime is the best form for the garden because it is safe and easy to buy and handle. If tests show that an application is needed, then at least six weeks must be allowed to elapse between farmyard manuring and liming, and at least a month between liming and the application of a chemical fertilizer. Lime should be applied to the surface of the soil in the spring just prior to planting.

Mulching

Now on to mulching trees and deeper-rooted shrubs, as I suggested earlier, the aim being to delay evaporation. This should be done during the spring and summer months, but the soil must be thoroughly wet after a downpour of rain or a good soak from the hose.

Peat is the ideal, but hop manure, vegetable refuse, lawn mowings (provided the lawn has not been treated with a hormone weedkiller) and any rotting material can be used, though such a mulch should not be deeper than two inches, otherwise in all cases other than peat a dangerous heat will be generated.

Spread out your mulch in a generous circle, remembering that roots are likely to extend as far as the branches of the tree. If the diligent earthworm is encouraged in this way, it will tug the mulch downwards into the earth, and do the work for you.

The Compost Heap

This larder is a veritable boon if there is room for it, and it brings tears to the eyes of the real gardener should potential compost material be wasted.

Refuse from the kitchen or garden in layers of three inches sandwiched between ordinary soil will make lovely garden compost in six months or so, helped along by a compost activator.

A few rules have to be kept. Keep your heap within five feet long, four feet wide and four feet high. Stack tidily, sloping the top, or covering it with polythene to avoid excessive moisture. A rustic or metal compost bin suitable for a town garden is now available from the sundriesman.

Turn sides to middle at half time (about three months). Avoid cabbage stumps (unless cut up), evergreen clippings and foliage, and wooden apple prunings that are slow to break down. Keep the heap moist but never allow it to get soggy.

Gardeners have their theories about compost heaps but agree that it is all-important that the heap should be well aerated. A few holes made with a pointed stick, pushed well into the heap, a month or so after the compost has reached a few feet will help to ensure that this is so.

Some gardeners hold the compost heap so dear that it is more sacred than the garden.

Digging

So much for additional soil conditioners and the right feed at the right time, but poor soil can be immensely improved by digging. There is a school of thought that holds that regular mulching can do away with the necessity of digging. This is, in many cases, wishful-thinking nonsense. In the majority of town gardens, few have the quantity of mulch that would be needed. But perhaps I should point out that there are successful suburban gardeners who have not dug their gardens since 1950. One man in particular, with a family and plenty of kitchen refuse, makes about $1\frac{1}{2}$ yds. of mulching material, which, plus peat and organic manures, satisfies a series of lovely plants.

Double digging is the ideal, but not everybody has the time or muscle to work two spades deep. Ordinary digging to the depth of the spit (or the spade) will let in the light, air and moisture and work wonders.

Drainage

Faulty drainage can be improved by trenching and filling the bottom of the trenches with clinkers, rubble and porous material that will absorb and help to clear the excess moisture.

Faulty drainage makes itself apparent by tell-tale pools of water that remain on the surface soil for a long period without dispersing, and dejected-looking plants that soon become demises.

The seriousness of the situation can be checked by digging two or three holes some 2 ft. deep on the site. If after heavy rain the holes remain half or more full of water for a considerable period, then some form of drainage system must be provided, to run into a main drain or soakaway.

But if water-logging is serious, then piping and a sump will be necessary and professional labour is best called in.

SOIL

Amenities

Garden amenities such as a greenhouse, cold-frame or shed must not be allowed to spoil the look of a garden. And it isn't much good trying to hide your greenhouse in a shady corner—because a greenhouse in the shade isn't worth a hoot unless you are a fern-lover.

Sheds are more easily camouflaged and in one season can be smothered by *Polygonum baldschuanicum*, and remain so until this rampant mile-a-minute, by sheer weight, brings the building down. It might be wiser to be rather more patient and grow a couple of less prolific but more distinguished climbers.

Then, of course, somewhere has to be found for the mower. I have known gardeners to pave a small garden because there was no place for the mowing-machine.

Again, space has to be found for the hose and room for the refuse bin. Some gardeners burn their rubbish and give the ashes to a treasured plant, but bonfires are sometimes difficult to arrange on a small estate. Half-a-crown to the dustman at pruning and clipping time is well worth while. Or with luck a handful of debris put into the bin day by day will pass unnoticed.

Having raised a series of devilish problems, I end this down-to earth chapter.

2 Design

Long, flat and uninteresting—easily measured in feet or maybe in yards—this is the uninspiring town garden that often falls to our lot. Oh, the dullness of it!

Every garden should be individual, so there can be no common formula to assist the beginner in carrying out the necessary transformation. He often makes the mistake of rushing off to a nursery and ordering a lot of plants instead of drawing up a simple, careful line-sketch of the garden-to-be. At this stage, his preferences for shrubs and plants are very secondary in importance to the layout.

A garden seldom succeeds without a design, if not on paper, at least in somebody's head. It creates the pattern—line, spacing, rhythm, sequence and colour, and saves much slavery later on. The best designs are simple in balance—the truer the sketch in scale the more likely it is to come off. Perspective and scale are important and easier lost sight of in a small garden than in Windsor or Richmond Park.

Whenever possible the design should have a highlight to quicken the interest, serving as a climax or focal point. If this feature is to attract and hold attention, it must be outstanding—a splash of colour, an exciting planting, an exclamatory shrub or tree, or a statue or ornament are accents that break monotony. The planner must beware of too many accents; we all know the garden with too many distractions and too much going on.

Colour is in demand by the town gardener, but those with heavily shaded gardens have to learn to maintain interest by the different greens and textures provided by foliage plants.

Texture and Form

Whereas nearly all gardeners dash for colour, texture and form are too often overlooked. A too-extensive planting of any one texture becomes boring; the smooth and coarse-leaved, the hard and soft that quiver in the breeze, the dull and the lustrous and the madly glossy that glitter and sparkle, should be allowed to show one another off. The rugged oak, the dark trim topiary yew, and the graceful birch and others as decorative should be found suitable companions.

Textures are particularly telling in towns, and an over-planting of dark green ivy is not only monotonous but depressing, while a gay edging of *Stachys lanata*, the little Lamb's Ear, with its silver nap foliage surrounding a contrasting bed of shrubs, roses or perennials, will always do its best to cheer you up.

Of no less importance than colour and texture are shape and form; the plant's individual silhouette must be taken into account—tall or dumpy, dense or thin-growing, column or spire. Irregularities should be planned to give variation of line, a pyramid may be found a place next to a cone or global-shaped shrub—or perhaps a tall grower planted next to a cushiony subject, but according to plan and not to jumble. Gertrude Jekyll's Yucca in the herbaceous border taught us the value of this technique, but her contrasts were well-managed **for** she had no time for chance assortments.

It is not only **from** books but from well-designed gardens that the beginner should derive information and ideas. The smaller the garden, the more essential is it that it should be designed on the best possible lines.

Of all gardens that I know, Hidcote, Chipping Campden, Gloucestershire, stands pre-eminent as the perfect model.

Hidcote

In spite of an atmosphere of age this is not an old garden. Major Lawrence Johnston made his first planting in 1905.

Any town gardener in search of an idea to break up the monotony of his dull patch should stay his hand and his spade until he has visited Hidcote. There is so much in this Gloucestershire garden that is applicable to small distant gardens in Gloucester Road, Kensington, and so many hints to be snapped up free of charge.

It is, of course, almost impossible to reproduce the world-famous harlequin hedge of Yew, Box, Holly, Beech and Hornbeam—but the boring Green Privet can be mingled with the Gold, and who knows, the Beech and Copper Beech or clipped Hornbeam may grow from time to time for a townsman.

Hidcote will be found to be formal, yet informal, and none of the small gardens are too elaborate to spill an idea to a London or city dweller. The majestic hedges, the circle of iris garden around the Strawberry Tree, the stilt garden of clipped Hornbeams, the pillar garden of English Yew and the occasional topiary, the terrace garden with its delightful gazebo, the stream or pine garden, the rock bank or the Camellia corner, all have a different lesson to teach. This is a garden of restraint and surprises that will inspire you.

Major Johnston has shown us beyond all else the possibilities of not only breaking up garden levels, but breaking up the garden into small gardens all entirely different in character, while giving each the illusion of being complete and part of the whole.

He started with one fine Cedar, two clumps of Beeches, ten acres of field, a generous banking account, botanical wisdom, unlimited energy, optimism, and above all, imaginative and sensitive taste. It was in every way a good start.

Hidcote is often described as being a garden of the cottage type because annuals, perennials, roses and others are allowed to go their way together—to scramble, jumble and pack close, cheek to cheek, so that the earth is never seen. But the true cottage garden is more strictly ruled than this.

I would prefer to call Hidcote a hedge garden, for the six main portions into which it is divided depend for their isolation on these living walls. It is the hedges that give the atmosphere and frame each picture; it is they that charm us, enclose us, hold us or shut us in. It is they that provide the mystery and the magic.

Of course, the Gloucestershire views, superb backcloths, and a wandering stream helped the master hand. And now that the master hand has gone, there is every now and then a planting that goes astray—a less successful choice of plants and a sad sense of the absence of the creator of the garden.

However, never let imitation wean you from your devotion to a particular plant or planting. Personal preferences, provided the subject has no aversion to the soil, should be given full play. Real gardeners have deep-seated likes and dislikes and are slow to change their minds. And after all, few plants are utterly dull if they are in the right company and place.

There are a thousand, thousand ways of making a garden. There is the formal, the symmetrical, stylized, artificial, yes, and the unnatural design.

There are those who will pepper their lawn with crescents and circles, those who favour spotty plantings of Lobelia and Alyssum that make one look away. There are plants and plantsmen with too many rarities and too little taste, and there are those who dare much, striving after a wild garden, the most elusive garden of all, where the mystery of the dell and wood and the violets and ferns so often escapes, however cosseted, and dies away. The wild garden is a possibility perhaps in a country town, but not in an area of smog.

There are the sensitive who will take into account the play of light and shade and the casting of shadows, and imaginative gardeners like Miss Bridget Boland, whose garden of illusion in Thurloe Square, South Kensington—although something of a gimmick—is a spoof that comes off.

The Garden of Illusion

On her return from a ten-year stay in Rome, Miss Boland found her twenty-foot-square garden a trifle frustrating. She designed an Italianate piece of wrought iron to fit and frame the ivied wall at the bottom of the garden and then placed three sheets of mirror glass each six feet high and two feet wide behind the arches. The effect is fascinating.

The sunken pool, the fountain and the gay beds of pastel petunias in a central position of the garden are admirably reflected in the looking-glasses.

Mirrors and gimmicks in a garden can be vulgar or amusing; they can also create desirable length and depth in a short garden and if the *trompe l'oeil* is well done, then it is fun to be taken in by such a phantom.

There is no doubt Miss Boland is an adventurous gardener, employing Impatiens or humble Busy Lizzie particularly well. She has a charming border of these, moving from the palest pink to the brash brick-reds and magentas. Within view of her semi-basement she has built up a bank where pots and plants can be lodged—and here again Busy Lizzie is given a good showing. This is a novel and excellent way of presenting the semi-basement dweller with colour and a hobby.

The garden of illusion is not to everybody's taste and it is certainly not for those who shrink at the idea of linking the artificial with nature—but it is inventive and a pleasant change.

Passing By

Designs and features in other people's gardens come to my mind as I write. A difficult corner skilfully handled with a bank and a beautifully planted wall; an old iron gate at the end of a path through which flowering shrubs could be seen led the eye onward to a further garden that was not there; a shining Holly hedge overrun with the Scotch Flame Flower, *Tropaeolum speciosum*, that was specially designed to be seen from a bedroom window—a clever adaptation of a design from a large garden reduced and made to fit a suburban slice; a rose garden of madder and violet species against a background of pleached Hornbeams.

Where the basic design is good, shrubs, plants and bulbs may come and go, but the garden will remain unimpaired.

Only when the motif is determined should the gardener decide to plant.

3 Walls, Windbreaks and Screens

The first walls I came across in my gardening career were of pink brick and were built about 1830. They were in my father's garden in Berkshire and enclosed a kitchen garden, and were decorated with pink blossom in the spring and peaches and nectarines in the summer. The sun could not always have been shining, but I remember the fruits as hot and luscious.

The second wall that came my way was built about the same time but it was black, and this time in my own garden in Holland Park, London. Blank and standing as it did at the end of the strip-domain—it looked grimly final. The bottom of the wall was the happy hunting-ground of an army of snails.

Haunted by the ugliness of this hideous structure, I rushed off to a nursery, came home with half-a-dozen climbers and planted them straightaway. This was my mistake. I should have whitewashed or painted the wall first.

The climbers grew fast and well, and although I often threatened to take them down and give them a clean white background, I never had the heart to disturb the *Solanum crispum*, that attractive member of the potato family with clusters of purple-blue flowers and pronounced yellow-orange stamens, for fear of losing it.

Wash or Paint

White walls, painted or whitewashed, have a magical effect in lightening their surroundings. Unfortunately, they soon lose their freshness in a built-up area, but covered with climbers their grubbiness becomes less noticeable.

All that is needed is a lick and a promise, and if the shape of the bricks shows through the paint or wash, so much the better. The same treatment is helpful in toning down a new, brash-red brick structure.

Happily, the brightening effect of painting our grimy city bricks has caught on and one comes across white, cream, pink, yellow and orange walls. A sensitive artist-gardener grows cream *Magnolia grandiflora* against a midnight-blue background, while a less sensitive politician trains the orange-berried Pyracantha against an unsympathetic backcloth of Suffolk pink.

Support for the Climbers

When it comes to deciding how to support the climber there are alternatives.

The plant can be trained to a trellis or wide-meshed netting fixed in panels against the wall, or parallel wires about a foot apart can be run across the wall, held by rust-proof loops driven into the mortar or cement, or by wall nails with flexible attachments that can be twisted round the shoot to be supported.

Of these, I believe that the parallel wires are the best method, causing less disturbance to the patient when pruning and training are undertaken. The installation of the loops for the wire is not easy and is best done by someone with the right tools, if not a professional.

The annuals Morning Glory, *Cobaea scandens* (the Cup-and-Saucer Plant, best grown as an annual) and the Canary Creeper appreciate a wide wire mesh.

The Dry Wall

Small dividing and terrace walls laid of loose stone without mortar or cement to bind them are known as dry walls. The stones must be carefully staggered so that they tie together and the wall given a slight backward tilt for stability.

Soil should be spread between the stones when the wall is made so that it can be planted up with rockery and alpine subjects. If the planting can be done when the wall is being built, so much the better.

24

Perhaps it should be pointed out that the dry wall must not be expected to hold and control any great weight of soil. Mortar or cement and maybe buttresses are required to withstand the burden of a terrace.

The Fruit Wall

Fruit trees on walls are decorative and often thrive in London, in particular the pear in the neighbourhood of St John's Wood.

Walls for fruit should be at least 6 ft. high, otherwise the tree's branches, shooting up above them, wave in the air, giving an uncomfortable appearance and robbing the lower branches of both growth and fruit.

Fruit trees grown flat against a wall and trained horizontally save space and simplify spraying and pruning.

The Port-hole

On occasion, a wall may block a view, in which case a round port-hole window can be cut and made a feature. The modern architect often develops this idea, providing the gardener with two independent gardens, two walls for climbers and an amusing peephole.

Such a garden was shown at the Royal Chelsea Show in 1966 by the County Borough of Southend-on-Sea.

The Open Garden

Whereas the majority of householders are jealous of their privacy, there are a few who dismiss hedges and walls in favour of an open front garden. Their emerald lawn marching flush with the public pavement is a tempting invitation to the stray dog and is only too often accepted by a varied pack of hounds. They, and the ghastly rubbish that blows in, destroy any feeling of extra space.

Windbreaks

Windbreaks are of vital importance to the roof and windswept garden. In certain circumstances a screen can be as helpful as a solid wall that merely deflects the blast over the brickwork—while permitting it to descend in unabated force a few yards the other side of the wall, resulting in a back current or whirl-blast.

Trees and shrubs that provide a decorative windbreak are a long-term proposition, making temporary screens a necessity. Among those to be considered are the wattle or woven-lap fencing, or board fences, horizontal or vertical. These permit a gentle flow of air between the boards but are a defence from the gales. The loose wattle fence has the advantage of looking right in almost any garden.

It is impossible to exaggerate the importance of windbreaks to a new garden. Plants will show their appreciation, the strong as well as the fragile, in a matter of weeks.

The Ornamental Screen

Inside garden screens are useful in dividing one part of the garden from another and give protection from the wind. They can be made of pre-cast pierced concrete blocks, U, V or fancy-shaped ridge tiles, the choice depending on the purpose of the screen.

The clairs-voyés pattern suits the small courtyard, provided the owners are not given to stripped sunbathing.

York and light Portland stone and various material screen walling blocks are to be had in different sizes (five to nine blocks to the square yard) in cement and ceramics, in as many as six colours. Of these I particularly like the hexagonal mesh completed by pink old brick piers.

Trellis and Light Screen Protection

Prefabricated trellis gives a garden, patio, courtyard, roof-top or balcony an established look, protection from prying eyes, and a lodging for the climbers. It is cheap and good value.

Climbers, flowering and others, can be bought from the garden centre at any time of the year, and planted without disturbance will soon give the screen a nicely dressed appearance.

Trellis can be mounted on a stone wall, above wattle or osier hurdles in order to give extra height.

A foliage-covered trellis is a more effective defence against the wind than one would suspect and has the advantage of reducing the influx of fumes, dust and dirt. Eyesores or undesirable views can be masked in sheltered places by a bamboo-cane curtain—at least during the summer months.

Netting wire or plastic is ideal for annuals, and of course the smaller the mesh the greater the protection.

The Shrub Screen

Long deep troughs of *Chamaecyparis lawsoniana* or conifers planted in deep boxes give a patio a feeling of maturity.

Roses such as 'Queen Elizabeth' or perhaps Forsythia against a chestnut fencing will make a splendid 5-6 ft. windbreak.

Fruit trees, on dwarfing stocks, if so wished can be used to divide one part of the garden from another or as a defence against the prevailing wind.

A garden in St John's Wood, London, has been planned in this way and espalier-trained apples make a delightful background to *Lilium regale, speciosum, auratum* and others.

The Mobile Screen

Screens of all kinds can be mounted on castors and made mobile. This suits owners who enjoy a change of scene and delight in moving garden furniture, containers and plants around.

The idea is to follow the sun—and seek shade from excessive heat; but it is a restless and tiring business.

Wall Collection Suitable for growing in or on Dry Walls

Alyssum saxatile 'Dudley Neville'
Aubrietia 'Dr Mules'
Campanula Birch Hybrid
Dianthus gratianopolitanus
Gypsophila repens
Helianthemum rhodanthe carneum

Hippocrepis comosa
Linaria alpina and *rosea*
Phlox lilacina 'Sensation'
Polygonum vaccinifolium
Saponaria ocymoides
Veronica prostrata 'Mrs Holt', and others.

4 Terrace and Paths— Pavings and Gravel

Eighteenth-century Capability Brown was the prime mover in abolishing the paved terrace, bringing the turf right up to the house —but he was dealing with great houses and parks and not the suburban or town house with its limited slice of garden.

It is interesting to note that it was this great landscaper who cut down many of the lovely avenues in this country because he disapproved of straight lines, and banished the entire vegetable garden into 'outer darkness'.

Avenues, the paved terrace, and vegetable gardens are now back in fashion, but the grass terrace is giving way to stone, crazy paving, cement, bricks, tiles, gravel or one of the many new paving materials that have been introduced during the last few years.

These materials are an answer to the townsman's prayer. He is weary of the hand mower and the calamity lawn with its bare patches and frayed edges, and with a sigh of relief says good-bye to his turf and generously gives away his mower.

Laying Paving

This is a mason's job, so gardener beware! The damp course must be located before work on the terrace is begun, for it is vital that the paving is sited below the damp course, otherwise the wet will seep into the house.

The foundation of consolidated hardcore, ashes and a generous supply of broken brick, must be rammed down firm and level in the main but sloped towards a drain if puddles are not to stay on the terrace and paths, making them unusable. A layer of finely sifted soil or sand should then be spread on the foundation and the stones placed in position.

If paving stones or slabs are to be stable then they must be laid on a solid foundation and bedded in 2 ins. of mortar mixture. Stones that rock as you tread on them are madly irritating, and dangerous.

Pockets can be left for small paving plants, the Saxifrages, Sedums and Thymes, or there can be one or two larger pockets for specimen shrubs or a small tree.

If the stones are left unpointed then the gardener must be prepared to weed between the stones, for the wind makes a business of blowing grass, daisy and plantain seed into terrace crevices.

The gardener pressed for time would be wise to confine his paving planting to a minimum so that he can dismiss weeds with an annual application of weedkiller. There is a great deal to be said for the well-swept weed-free terrace that relies on decorative containers filled with suitable plants for colour and interest.

Those who find courtyard or terrace paving and concrete slabs a trifle monotonous may consider introducing alternate or occasional squares of turf, Thyme or Chamomile, while realizing that adventurous designs nearly always entail extra work.

When it comes to choosing paving there is marble for the rich and pebble-dash and chippings for those with less to spend, and a great choice in between.

Paving Stones

York paving is the Rolls-Royce of pavings but rather expensive.

Second-hand paving stones, suitable for town gardens, are to be had on occasion. Well weathered by time and town atmosphere, they readily fit into any surroundings, and have the advantage of being reasonably cheap. Unfortunately they are apt to vary in thickness and therefore are best professionally laid if an even surface is to be achieved. It is important that the stones are carefully squared and coursed precisely, whatever the pattern decided upon. Different lengths are permissible so long as they do not lead to a confusion of disorderly joints that are the hallmark of the amateur.

Concrete

This is the decade of concrete; it is serviceable and cheap. Fortunately, the concrete industry has taken the material in hand and dismissed its austerity, and it now presents the formal effect of paving stones. There are pre-cast hydraulically pressed concrete flags, and pre-cast slabs with rougher surface textures that not only make them non-slip but improve their appearance generally. By using two types of surface finishes combined, and different shades of concrete, endless patterns can be designed.

. Colouring is mixed with the concrete and slabs are to be had in six or more colours. The dark coloured and black pavings will be found less glare-making than those in the lighter shades.

Concrete slabs of various makes are available in $1\frac{1}{2}$-3 in. thickness and different sizes. The hexagonal paving is particularly attractive, as indeed are the concrete stepping-stones or circular paving slabs for the lawn.

The do-it-yourself man must see to it that the concrete is well mixed, otherwise it will weaken, resulting in the paths being in need of constant repair.

Crazy Paving

Always described as 'informal', crazy paving can be had in Purbeck, Somerset, York and Pennant stone, Cornish and Westmorland slate and broken concrete slab.

These jagged broken stones put together in a somewhat maladroit pattern are cheap but seldom satisfying.

Brick Pavings

Old bricks, warm and friendly in character, are delightful for paving terraces, courtyards and paths.

I like some of the modern bricks too, such as Lunsford Blue Brown Bricks and the dull ochre to purplish-brown Wealden rough stocks.

All these make excellent paving surrounds for large shrubs or a young tree. If the joints are left unsealed and filled with chippings, the rain can percolate and the inner ring of bricks can be removed as the tree grows.

Bricks can be laid longwise or across in basket-weave pattern. Old bricks are ideal for laying traditional herring-bone paths, and if stood up on end and sloping, make useful edgings.

A solid foundation rolled to the required fall for the bricks must be prepared, and the bricks laid on a bed of sand or lime. Plants can be encouraged in the joints: the colour of the sand should be chosen with care to match with the bricks. The growth of lichen and moss can be encouraged and gives an atmosphere of age.

Slate, Tiles, Cobbles, Pebbles and Chippings

Olive-green to blue-purple and reddish slates from Westmorland to Cornwall have their charm, and are successfully used by architects and designers as borders to other materials.

Terrazzo tiles that will outlast you are another suggestion, while quarry tiles in heather and other mixtures seem to have come into fashion since they were used in Coventry Cathedral.

Cobbles on edge or flat make fascinating patterns if the layer has the gift and the time to copy the radiating designs of the eighteenth century.

Pebbles, pebbledash kept under control, and chippings can be pleasant if the design is restful rather than fussy.

Gravel

The great advantage of gravel is that it can be put down on awkward levels, is easy to lay, and will last ten years or so. But the gravel courtyard and paths must be well drained, otherwise it will stick to shoes and come into the house with you. There is the added annoyance of chairs and seats that get stuck and unmanageable if the surface is soggy.

Maintenance is light and the occasional use of a roller or rake, and weedkiller will usually fill the bill. Greening by algae can be quickly halted by a watering with domestic bleach.

Gravel planted in imaginative designs with small box edging is simple but engaging.

Paving Collection Suitable for inserting in Holes in Paved Walks

Acaena buchananii
Arenaria caespitosa aurea
Cotula squalida
Erigeron mucronatus
Frankenia thymifolia
Houstonia caerulea
Lysimachia minuta

Paronychia amanus
Pratia angulata
Raoulia glabra
Saxifraga hypnoides var. densa
Thymus sepyllum coccineus
Veronica pectinata rosea

A garden on the street in the city of Norwich

Small back garden in Palmers Green designed by John Brookes.
L. to r. Flowering Rheu, *Fatsia japonica* and Miscanthus. The head
was rescued from the ruins of the local cinema

5 Patio and Roof Garden

The patio is an inner courtyard open to the sky. Romans, Arabs, Persians, Spaniards, Mohammedans, Americans and now the British have in turn been fascinated by this portico court-house.

The most glamorous patio I have seen was in Jos, Nigeria, where an old Frangipani bent over the wall and with the palest of Bougainvilleas provided the shade; the oasis was brilliant with small orchids and heavy with the Frangi's scent: the sun was shining but there was shade, and the fountain was graceful and only gently splashing. The patio-maker is half way there if he has the sun.

We have learned a great deal recently from the Americans about underfloor electric heating making the patio habitable during the autumn and the springtime, if not the whole year round.

A sliding glass screen that I saw in New York is ideal for patio, terrace or roof-garden. It was of frameless plate glass panels of 4 and 7 ft. tall and obviously expensive, the huge plates swinging noiselessly over each other. But framed glass panels, light and mobile and made to pack away against the wall, are practical and much cheaper.

Transparent plastic set in a sturdy wood frame on castors heavy enough not to blow over is easy to move as the wind changes, but alas, not so good-looking.

Trellis, often looked upon as purely decorative, will be found helpful in defeating the prevailing wind: but gay, brightly-coloured canvas screens and awnings that give a Riviera look are not weather-proof and are quick to fade.

If the extension is to be used throughout the year there must be some form of paving, and preferably some form of roofage, if only pergola joists or battens of cedar wood. Polished sheets of glass, wired for safety, will if the patio is heated enable the owner to keep an even temperature.

Once a steady warmth can be provided, even the temperamental house plants can be brought out for a short stay. Eucalyptus, the Blue Gum, used for summer bedding (sown in August and grown on under glass for planting out the following summer), makes a striking background plant. If you have a greenhouse and green fingers to go with it, red and yellow-green *Poinsettia mikkelsen* will make an exciting planting against the Gum's glaucous foliage.

Quite a lush effect is to be had from the fig family, the Aphelandra, and our old friend the variegated Aspidistra, lit up here and there by a dashing florist's plant—a bright Azalea or Gloxinia—a Saintpaulia group—or perhaps a pot of Marigolds or sweet-scented Stocks. Purists who prohibit roses in their herbaceous border or annuals among their houseplants miss a great deal.

If the patio is unheated and there is good ventilation, then the Passion Flower, the Hoya, *Cobaea scandens*, Black-Eyed Susan (*Thunbergia alata*), Lapageria, roses and others will enjoy the glass protection.

Patio lighting requires careful wiring, and an armoured electric cable, which is advised for safety, will be found long-lasting. Garden flood-lighting can be very beautiful and a spotlight trained on a well-grown tree will give it a fairy-like glamour. Spotlights should be hidden and controlled by indoor switches to encourage the illusion.

Lanterns, fairy lights, pillar-mounted lamps and disused lamp-posts are much sought after, while carriage-lamps have for many years been on the list of those who collect Victoriana.

When it comes to furniture the practical will go for table book-case, cupboards, bar or barbecue and sophisticated amenities—while the more primitive will depend for décor upon their oiled and well-tanned bodies stretched out on a chaise-longue.

Pomegranates, Passion Fruit and flowering Oleanders would be lovely, but alas, are seldom happy in England.

The Roof Garden

Drinks on the roof is an invitation with a happy, cool, summer ring, even if the roof garden only entails a couple of Russian vines, the mile-a-minute climbers, twisting their way round a trellis and a couple of chimneys.

Before taking action, the opinion of a surveyor or architect should be sought to find out the maximum weight of soil the roof can safely carry.

The keynotes of a successful roof-top are much the same as those of the patio garden, but of course, on this occasion, you have a view without a background—an enormous expanse of sky, sun without shade, and more often than not, a howling wind. This makes the protection of screens and windbreaks a necessity.

The roof garden has possibilities, but its success will depend more than any other on its owner's imagination. Four borders round the perimeter and a diamond bed in the centre is as dull a layout upstairs as it is below.

Brick-built troughs (if the roof will carry them) and large crates that will hold a generous amount of soil are best for the permanent small tree or shrub—they should be 12-16 ins. deep for resident plants, and 12-18 ins. wide.

Soil

There is already a chapter on this subject, but because roof soi dries out so quickly the gardener is advised to give his more per-nickety plants lashings of peat that will hold the moisture; a bag or two of leaf-mould brought home in the car from the country will be appreciated, as will a liberal basic dressing of very coarse bonemeal, plus any kitchen bones available.

Roof-garden plants require fairly constant feeding: a liquid fertilizer will act as a quick pick-me-up if there is a party in the offing. Permanent shrubs will need frequent top-dressing.

Drainage and Watering

All containers should have drainage holes and these must be covered with an extra thick layer of roughage to ensure a fast runaway. They should, whenever possible, be lifted an inch or so from ground level so that there is no danger of the drainage holes being blocked.

Troughs and tubs must in no way interfere with the ordinary roof drainage and leaves and debris must be regularly collected to pre-vent obstruction.

Having provided a fast runaway, it will be necessary to water the garden once or even twice a day in dry weather. Roof gardens, balconies, window-boxes and hanging baskets dry out quickly and must be carefully watched.

Piping and a hose are important amenities, otherwise can-carrying becomes exhausting. A New York landscaper told me he was planning an automatic spray for his roof garden that could be turned on from his bedside, but I have not yet heard how this turned out. A simple mist irrigator is now on the British market and would be ideal for this purpose.

Plants

Shrubs and small trees require a secure anchorage in deep troughs or large pots if they are to survive the winter. Those chosen should be absolutely hardy, and young Chestnuts, Figs and mini fruit trees in tubs are worth considering.

When it comes to perennial herbaceous plants, mini border, ground-huggers and creepers have an advantage over tall plants. Staking must be tactfully carried out and the foliage allowed to hide the sticks.

Annuals that enjoy the sunshine and light grow well in pots and are easily slipped out when they have finished flowering. Nasturtiums and in particular pink 'Cherry Rose' can be used effectively, as well as Forget-me-nots, Polyanthus, Lobelia, Pansies and Petunias in variety if a fine summer is predicted.

Bulbs can be relied upon to give their usual spring performance on the roof. Small bulbs such as the Snowdrop, Aconite, Crocus and Scilla can stand up to the wind, as indeed does the stocky-stemmed Hyacinth.

Daffodils and Tulips should be selected for stoutness of stem and inconspicuously supported by short twiggy sticks.

The brilliant *Tulipa praestans* 'Fusilier' with two or three flaming scarlet blooms on each stem, pale-yellow small-flowered *batalinii*, with creeping ribbon-like leaves only 4 inches high, and brilliant *greigii* with attractively marked foliage and some of the dwarf forms of Water-lily *kaufmanniana* are all gems for protected corners.

Among the daffodils, the strong-stemmed Tazetta 'Cheerfulness', 'Geranium' or 'Scarlet Gem' will brighten any dull niche.

36

Lastly there are the all-important climbers. Among them, the magnificent *Ampelopsis hederacea*, now known as *Parthenocissus quinquefolia*, and the Virginia Creeper that gives a short spell of intense autumn brilliance. The star-like *Clematis montana*, the vigorous winter yellow or the summer white Jasmine, and of course *Polygonum baldschuanicum*, the rampant Russian vine with panicles of lush white flowers.

Grass can be grown on the roof, and I was shocked to hear from the Continent that plastic grass is now to be had by the yard for this purpose.

Herb gardens are popular with the cook, on the roof or in the area, while Tomatoes, Parsley and Chives can be grown by salad-lovers.

Folly Formula

Roof gardens should be a mixture of gardening and folly, *trompe l'oeil*, murals, pools and fountains, amusing garden furniture or perhaps a graceful and decorative ornament, a modern abstract or a romantic statue, or just a topiary bear in a tub.

Plants and Shrubs Suitable for Roof Gardens
(Recommended by Mr. L. A. Russell)

Acuba japonica varieties
Azalea obtusa (Kurume) varieties
Berberis buxifolia
B. thunbergii atropurpurea
B. t. a. nana 'Little Favourite'
Bergenias, various—in particular cultivars
Cotoneaster horizontalis
C. microphyllus
C. salicifolia 'Autumn Fire' and others
Fatsia japonica
Hebe (*Veronica*) *albicans*
H. anomala

H. × *edinensis*
H. sub-alpina
Hederas, various
Pernettyas, various
Potentilla 'Gibson's Scarlet'
Prunus laurocerasus schipkaensis
P. l. zabelliana
Pyracanthas, various

Rhododendrons large-flowered hardy hybrids
  'Britannia'
  'Doncaster'
  'Gomer Waterer'
Sedum 'Autumn Joy'

37

The success of these plants depends on the surrounding draught protection.

H. 'Autumn Glory'

H. buxifolia

S. spectabile 'Carmen'

Senecio (shrubby species)

Spiraea densiflora

Syringa palabiniana

Mr H. Taylor adds a few others to the above

Common Fig

Elaeagnus

Euonymus

Hosta

Olearia haastii

Tamarix

Yucca

6 The Garden on Different Levels

The town builder leaves the garden flat as if it were in his contract to do so, with the result that the suburban garden plot is pancake level. Any hummocky garden that survives is quickly levelled out by its owner, either by hand or bulldozer. It is his first big job.

So the thousands of little front gardens that border the arterial roads, bubbling over with beautiful roses all the summer, are as flat as the gardeners can make them.

And because the garden is flat in front, later on it is likely that it will be flat behind. This is a great pity and opportunities are lost.

It is often complained that the modern landscape architect has given us little new, but I am particularly grateful to the designer who inspired us to garden on different levels. I have not been able to discover his name.

The emphasis on different depths and elevations, the sunken garden on two or more levels and the raised bricked-in bed are effective ways of increasing the sense of space, giving a lift to the design in more ways than one.

The Raised Bed

The first successful stepped herbaceous border that I came across was at the International Gartenbau Ausstellung, Hamburg, in 1963.

It was cleverly undulated and the change of levels gave the beds particular interest, inconspicuous plants being brought to notice while the brasher subjects were kept in place.

There were cut-step terraces on high banksides that enabled the

39

gentians and small plants to show themselves off in a spectacular way. But beyond the new variations in planting value there were other benefits. Drainage was automatically improved by raising the level of soil. Pinks, Iris that like their rhizomes baked in the sun, and others with an aversion to the damp benefit by the faster runaway, while 'the lift' in a dark corner leads to more light and air, which suits the majority of plants.

This up-and-down border should also be a blessing to the gardener with an unsuitable figure for bending.

I came home to find the long borders at Southport, and Kensington Gardens, though as lovely as ever, a trifle boring.

The Raised Brick Bed

The raised brick bed built in careful proportions is particularly successful in a front garden of the handkerchief variety. Need it be said that, like all containers, it needs good drainage, plenty of roughage and constant watering in dry weather.

Here is an opportunity of cosseting a shrub or plant that does not like your particular soil. Gardeners on lime will be able to fill the brick-raised bed with peat and leaf-mould and confidently plant Rhododendrons, Azaleas and other acid-loving subjects that have been impossible to grow before.

In Hamburg the elevated soil was retained by formal curved walls. These could be of brick, stone, cement or peat blocks. Two small walls rather than one large one will be found more satisfactory when using peat blocks and the support strengthened by adding a border of bricks laid crossways on the top of the lower wall.

Steps

The garden on two levels is best linked by a flight of steps, but even two or three will give an illusion of space. Shallow steps fit into the garden better than steep ones and the treads are excellent spots for containers and pots.

The riser below the tread looks attractive when planted with a dark small-leaved ivy so long as it is kept tidy and in place.

Warning

Avoid a single step and the need for warning or apologizing to visitors for its presence.

Soil should never be built up nor removed below ordinary ground level round the bole of a tree. Many a beautiful veteran oak has been killed in this way or slowly murdered by a thick blanket of lawn mowings.

7 Containers

There has been a wind of change in plant containers, due very largely to the arrival of the garden centre.

We now come home from this modern nursery with a plant more often than not in a temporary container, a plastic sleeve, tin can or something of the kind. A new home and holder has to be found for the plant if it is not to be planted directly in the garden.

These container-grown plants can be slipped into the ordinary clay pot and this method satisfies the large army of flower-pot gardeners.

Pots enable the gardener to give plants individual attention and a special diet, but particular care must be taken in the summer that they do not dry out. In a very hot summer or during the owner's absence they can be sunk in damp peat—or a pot can be slipped into a larger pot and the margin between the two filled with moist peat or dampened moss.

Unusual containers, perhaps an amusing piece of junk, are fun so long as they have drainage holes.

The Clay Pot

I like the clay pot, its look, its colour and the feel of it. Beginners are often bedevilled by the variety of its sizes. The number given denotes the number of pots that can be made out of a cast, hence the smaller the size the higher the number. The depth of the pot is about the same measurement as the diameter. There are 72 small 'thumbs' and eight 12-in. pots to the cast; and the clays can be bought by the dozen along with saucers if wanted.

Nurserymen very naturally are turning to plastic pots, for they are easily and quickly scrubbed and are unbreakable. Beyond this, plants in plastic pots dry out slower than those in clay, which means they need less watering.

Italian Terra-cotta

These are my favourite containers, Venetian or Florentine, whether the small plain pot with its rounded lip or the large highly decorative 'Vaso' with its delightful swag reliefs.

I have used the troughs for many years for window-box gardening and my one regret is that they do not allow more space for planting so that the gardener can slip a plant out of a 40 pot and, without disturbing the root ball, drop it into the trough.

However, the Corregio box and the many different types of jardinières are ideal for bulbs and summer bedding plants and look lovely filled with Ivy-leaved Geraniums.

The tall terra-cotta jars are desirable garden ornaments for terraces or the tread of a step, but I have failed to find a plant that looks happy or in proportion held in their restricting necks. However, it will be found that even unplanted the distinguished jar gives a certain atmosphere.

Concrete and Asbestos Boxes

The low flat bowls that made their first appearance at County Hall during the Festival of Britain in 1951 were an immediate success. We invested in six of these for the London square in which I live. They are usually planted with brilliant 'Red Emperor' Tulips in the spring and salmon-pink 'King of Denmark' Geraniums in the summer. The advantage of such containers is that they can be placed in a sunny spot, and as they hold a generous number of plants, can be relied on to make a real splash. This flat patterned bowl has come to stay.

Other concrete-designed troughs such as the Ben Hur cast with chariot and galloping horses are good, while the asbestos Urastone boxes, plain, fluted, ribbed or draped, are cheap and long-lasting. Although of an uninteresting grey, they can be gaily painted.

Fibreglass

Fibreglass urns and tanks are perfect copies of the eighteenth-century lead, having been taken from the original moulds. They are surely the élite containers, but they are not cheap. Strong, resistant and frost-proof, they are as light as a feather. They look very much at home on old brick piers, and weathered pink walls.

Plastic

There is a series of plastic containers such as the insulant Jablite ledge-box of expanded polystyrene.

The advantage of Jablite is that the products retain heat, with the result that the soil can be kept at a more constant temperature, entailing less watering. They are to be had in a series of colours and are available from the sundriesman.

Anyone considering containers of this kind should visit Rassell's of 80 Earl's Court Road, Kensington, London, W.8., where there is a wide range of pots, troughs and tubs on view.

Wood

Wooden containers, readily available and easy to make, are the most common in use. They are a wise choice for a hot sunny position, evaporation of moisture being slower in the wood tub than the earthenware.

Wine and beer casks are easily converted into tubs, galvanized iron hoops if present being allowed to stay. Drainage holes must be made and the inside of the tub treated with Cuprinol (S.Q.D.) or a safe bituminous paint. Charring the inside of containers is an alternative for the active and responsible.

White tubs always look right in the garden. But I have a picture in mind of dark blue tubs standing on a terrace, some filled with *auratum* Lilies and others with blue Agapanthus.

Large trees that are to remain in place for a number of years are difficult to keep going unless the sides and the bottom of the container can be removed and the trees fed with fresh soil.

The cube Versailles *caisses* seen outside the large French châteaux or such British houses as Merriworth Castle, Maidstone, hold veteran orange trees. These dignified containers have side panels that slot in and out and in many cases two slides are removed each spring, the tired soil being rubbed away to make place for fresh and stimulating compost, thus enabling an orange tree to survive for decade after decade.

Any number of shrubs can be grown in large containers provided they are given good soil to their taste, are top-dressed at least once or twice a year and occasionally fed.

I suggest a few subjects but by no means attempt a complete list of suitable plants.

Shrubs

Acer (Japanese Maple)
Camellia
Chaenomeles (Japanese Quince)
Fatsia japonica
Hydrangea
Lavender

Magnolia (*M. soulangeana, M. stellata*)
Rhododendron
Rose
Rosemary
Sweet Verbena
Yew

Bulbs and Corms

Hyacinth, Narcissi, Tulips interplanted with Crocus, Grape Hyacinths and Scillas are most effective when planned to fall in with the window-box colour scheme, either matching or pleasantly contrasting with them.

Lilium regale

Gladioli (Primulinus)—under 3 ft.

Herbaceous Plants

Acanthus
Agapanthus
Fuchsia

Hosta
Iris
Pelargoniums

Annuals

Antirrhinum

Marigold

Nasturtium

Phlox drummondii

Water-Lilies

Small concrete tanks or tubs of about 12 ins. in depth will make a happy home for a small water-lily such as *Nymphaea pygmaea alba* (white); *N. odorata minor* (white); *Laydekeri lilacea* (pink); and *Laydekeri fulgens* (crimson). If a water-lily tub is to be entertained, a water-garden nursery should be consulted.

The Strawberry Barrel

This container makes its return to fashion after a century's absence.

One end of the barrel has to be removed and 2-in. apertures made for the plants. These should not be positioned lower than 2 ft. from the base of the barrel: two floors of openings are advised for the small and three floors at most for the large barrel. Care must be taken that the openings alternate regularly storey by storey, with the result that those on the third floor are directly above those on the first floor.

A 2-in. perforated zinc tube should be inserted for watering. Care should be taken to sink it deep enough to serve the plants on the first floor.

Once the holes are planted up, four more strawberry plants may be installed in the top of the barrel.

A beer barrel of this kind is equally suitable for Houseleeks, Dianthus, Aubrietias, Saxifrages, Cambridge and Oxford blue Lobelias, and others. For some of these, larger holes of 4-6 ins. will be required.

Baskets

Hanging baskets are a charming way of decorating a porch and help to brighten the dullest of doorways. However, recently some local authorities have hung them high on lamp-posts, where they look out of proportion and on a windy day most unsafe. But don't let that put you off; baskets round the patio or hung just overhead on a roof garden can be most effective.

Wooden and wire patterns 12-18 ins. in diameter ready with chains for hanging are to be had from the sundriesman. A large basket, after watering, is heavy to handle and on a hot summer's day will have to be taken down for a soak both morning and evening.

A home-made potting compost of loam, leaf-mould and peat with a good sprinkling of sharp sand should be used, or John Innes No. 2 for the ordinary run of plants and No. 3 for the extra vigorous.

The container must be lined with moist sphagnum moss, followed by a layer of turfy loam, and examined to see that there is no opening where the soil can escape before the compost and plants are put in.

Baskets need firm planting and constant inspection to see that they do not dry out. The best way is to take the basket down and give it a thorough soak for fifteen minutes, remembering that the wind can be almost as drying as the sun.

An evening syringe should be a matter of routine, not only for dampening the foliage but for removing dust and dirt.

The choice of plants is a wide one, but trailing subjects that spill over the edge of the basket like a waterfall are the most successful. And here the Ivy-leaved Geranium and the Petunia are hard to beat.

Gardeners who prefer erect central plants for their basket will find Begonias excellent for a shady position, Heliotrope exceptional for scent, Marguerites summerlike and gay even if it is raining, and Fuchsias and Coleus fast and free-growing, while bright-blue Lobelia 'Mrs Clibran Improved' with a captivating white eye, can always be relied upon to hide the basket by tumbling over its edge.

The Wheelbarrow

The gaily painted garden barrow full of bedding plants in bloom is no longer a novelty, and on its way out. It was too gimmicky to last.

8 Ornaments for the Garden

The town garden, unlike the country garden, is not always spilling over with flowers and has to depend to some extent on interesting features outside the plant world. These focal points are excellent so long as there are not too many of them.

Sculpture is the answer for those who can afford it. Damaged pieces of sculpture have a particular charm of their own. A missing ear or nose means little in the garden, and the broken and limbless can often be picked up cheaply at auctions, markets or junk shops.

Lead urns, vases or figures are superb, but I regret to say that the small modern garden ornaments turned out by the garden artists of today seem to me rather poor stuff, while the gnomes, storks and others of that ilk are perfect horrors. I have in vain begged several young sculptors who produce immense and rather frightening figures that few can house to turn their attention to smaller fry to decorate our gardens. But alas, in spite of the tremendous potential market, no one comes forward.

I wonder, too, that among the thousands of amateur painters and would-be sculptors more of them do not turn their attention to enhancing the garden themselves.

At the late Sir Winston Churchill's home, Chartwell, John Churchill's murals are certainly entertaining and I see no reason why those who so fearlessly paint pictures should not paint walls.

A little home modelling in clay should also be encouraged, for even if not frost-resistant, who knows, a crack here and there might improve the ensemble, and if not, it can be covered by a rambler rose.

Meanwhile, we must content ourselves with what is available, such as mushroom-shaped staddle stones on which our forefathers

An amusing seat at University College, Oxford, designed by Sylvia Crowe

Paving and topiary.
A school courtyard
in Denmark
designed by Arne Jacobsen

Brick paving by Redland Bricks of Horsham.
The inner ring can be removed as the tree trunk thickens

stacked their ricks. These certainly help to keep cars off the grass and have a pleasant classical look.

There are sinks, much-sought-after old lamp-posts, della Robbias and endless sundials. Of these I prefer the very modern abstract patterns rather than the old-world dials that have a bogus look.

Garden furniture has taken on a new lease of life and can be a great asset so long as it is comfortable and weather resistant.

9 The Lawn

If a lawn is not properly made in the first place it seldom comes right. And as a groundsman said, 'If the grass isn't green, it's ghastly.'

The first decision that has to be taken when making a lawn is whether it is to be seeded or turfed.

Good seed from a reputable firm is better than the average turf available and it is cheaper. Preparation for seed or turf is the same. A depth of 10-12 ins. of soil capable of retaining moisture, a fine tilth, a feed with a balanced fertilizer and meticulous levelling are essential for the emerald sward.

Seed

Seed should be bought from a seed specialist with an eye to the particular soil, dry or damp, right for town sowing and the use for which the lawn is intended. If it is to stand up to hard wear, then the grass must be fairly coarse—if it has merely to be good-looking, then it can be delicate and fine.

Seed should be sown at the end of August, after the soil has been allowed to fallow and the weeds from the area removed. If 2 ozs. of seed per square yard are sown, the gardener can expect a good lawn by the autumn of the following year.

Turf

Turf must be bought from a reliable firm and inspection is advised before buying, looking for firmness, 2-in. thickness, good colour and grass quality.

Turf has the advantage that it can be laid at any time provided there is not a drought or frost. It must be watered generously and regularly if laid during a dry spring or summer and any seams that appear between the turves should be filled with finely-sifted compost.

Now on to after-care. And here I feel the most helpful thing I can do is to give a short monthly programme for lawn maintenance.

January. Brush away all fallen leaves. The grass should not be walked upon more than is necessary when it is sodden or frozen by frost. The sundriesman will be grateful if the gardener sends the mower to be serviced now rather than waiting until the spring rush.

Worm casts may appear during mild and damp days and these should be brushed away with a besom. If the sticky mounds are walked upon and flattened they will clog and damage the turf.

February. A moderate worm population will be found helpful in aerating the soil, but if the worms become troublesome this is the time to eradicate them.

The lawn should be dressed with a wormkiller with a mowrah meal basis and well watered in, whereupon the worms will rise in hundreds.

Sweeping up the corpses, an extremely unpleasant chore, is best done sooner than later.

March. For most gardeners, serious maintenance begins this month.

First the lawn should be given one or two thorough brushes with the besom to dismiss all debris. Aeration by slit or solid tine piercing and raking are all important in March and early April.

If you have a very light roller you may care to give the lawn one roll to put the frost-lifted turf back into place. The modern lawn specialists tell us to beware of the roller, and if not already in possession of one, to make do with the mower with the blades tipped so that they are out of service.

The roller should not weigh more than 2 cwts. and should **never** be used when the lawn is wet.

Limit the mowing to two cuts in March, raking with a spring-toothed rake between the two mowings so that the grass stands up to meet the blades. Set the blades high this month and just tip or top the grass. The new lawn should not be cut until 3 ins. high.

April. The first application of fertilizer should be given early this month; this can be either home-made or of a reputable make.

Here is a helpful recipe for spring use:

> 3 parts sulphate of ammonia
> 3 parts dried blood
> 4 parts superphosphate
> 4 parts boneflour
> 1 part sulphate of potash

Apply when the soil is moist at 2-3 ozs. per square yard.

The gardener with only a small garden will not find it worth while making up this many-itemed mixture. However a bag of Sustanum Grass Fertilizer (sold only in 28-lb. bags), Fortified Seaweed Manure, or Fison's Evergreen (a combined stimulant and weedkiller) will fill the bill.

Meanwhile, N.P.K. (nitrogen phosphate and potash in a well-balanced mixture) is always a useful spring general fertilizer.

Moss can be controlled by mercurized lawn sand but will inevitably return if the lawn is compacted, badly drained, impoverished, or very shady, and raking will merely scatter the spores, doing more harm than good. It may be necessary to instal pipes and a soakaway if the trouble is to be cured.

Mowing should be more frequent as the grass starts actively growing but still with the blades high, not cutting lower than an inch—any tufts of coarse grass should be removed by hand.

May. Mowing should proceed once a week at least, lowering the blades at the beginning of the month to three-quarters of an inch.

Weedkilling should now begin in earnest, using a lawn sand or perhaps a selective hormone killer to eliminate certain weeds. A dry, warm, windless day should be chosen with a look of rain in the sky. If there is no rainfall after the application, then the chemical must be watered in and the manufacturer's instructions followed to the letter if the turf is not to be burnt black-brown.

Regular and generous watering should be started if there is a spring drought and it is important that this should begin before the lawn has dried out. Dribs and drabs are not beneficial; the lawn should be given a good soaking and allowed to partly dry out before being soaked again.

Lawn fans will treat their turf to an early summer compound fertilizer. Others will content themselves with a spring and autumn programme.

June. Twice-a-week mowing should begin this month. Make a point of changing the direction with every cut. Mow along the length of the lawn at the first mowing, across at the next, and finally diagonally from corner to corner. In this way the coarse grass and weeds cannot escape the blades and the grass is encouraged to spread.

Weeding must go forward with weedkillers, hormones and by hand, using a spot killer against pearlwort and the more resistant weeds. The tufts of grass should be slashed with an edging iron, the clover raked up so that it meets the mower's blades and the daisies controlled with lawn sand or hormones.

Maybe the lawn will now benefit by a second feed—here is a recipe that can be used as a summer stimulant:

1 oz. nitro-chalk

4 ozs. sand

To be used at the rate of 1 oz. per square yard.

If for some reason immediate results are wanted, 1 oz. of potash nitro to a gallon of water over 12 square yards has a magical effect.

Or for acid soil, 1 oz. of nitro-chalk to 5 square yards is preferable.

High nitrogen fast-acting stimulants that encourage lush and susceptible growth should not be used after the end of July.

July. Regular mowing should go forward, avoiding close shaving, for the grass blades will shade the roots during a heat wave. If during holidays the lawn has grown long, it is wiser to remove this growth in two cuts rather than one, so that there is less shock to grass roots.

August. Go on with the good work, not allowing the weeds to reestablish themselves. Renovation and re-sowing of unsuccessful areas can be made towards the end of the month.

September. The mower's blades should be slightly raised from now onwards. The autumn is the time for spiking the lawn with a hollow-tined fork in order to improve drainage and help clay soils where the turf is over-compact and matted.

This is the time of year to give the hungry lawn an extra feed with a slow-acting bulk organic dressing, once again home-made or from a reputable horticultural firm. Here is a useful recipe for a late September to October application:

3 ozs. complete fish manure
8 to 16 ozs. compost or peat.

It should be applied to one square yard after spiking, then brushed in.

If on heavy soil, half compost and half sharp or coarse sand should be used.

Seaweed manure mixed equally with sieved compost at 3-4 ozs. per square yard is also helpful. Marinure is a good seaweed dressing and its seaside smell lasts for a few hours only. If the lawn is in good order and just needs a pick-me-up, a top-dressing of good loam, peat and sand finely sieved after the lawn has been spiked will fill the bill. Lawns on light soil should be dressed with a peat compost, while those on clay should be treated to a generous amount of sharp coarse sand.

Autumn is the time for carrying out repairs.

Small hollows can be levelled up by sprinklings of finely sieved compost until the area is sufficiently raised.

The turf must be rolled back from deep hollows and bumps, the soil added or removed and the turf replaced.

Bare and brown patches (maybe the trade-mark of a bitch) must be cut out and seeded or re-turfed.

Edgings should be trimmed and, where the sides have been trodden down or have crumbled, built up with a little extra soil, which can be removed in the spring when the grass has made good.

October. Mowing should gradually cease with the blades raised higher.

This is the month when toadstools, puff-balls and fairy rings

54

appear. The fairy ring, when brushed away, is apt to leave a tell-tale dark green circle and later a thin line of bare earth.

This is an invasion that can be persistent. The ring should be deeply spiked with a tine fork and well soaked with a solution of 2 ozs. of Epsom Salts to the gallon.

If the infected area fails to respond, there is nothing for it but to remove the affected turf and the soil below it, but care must be taken not to spill the soil when carrying out the operation as infection is easily spread.

November. Perhaps a last mow or two on a dry warm day. Leaves and any worm casts should be brushed away.

December. Brush the lawn occasionally and keep off the grass.

Where Paths Meet the Lawn

The rectangle lawn is the familiar lawn, turf and flatness often being immaculate, but paths patterned without a thought for design may well ruin the whole effect.

We must be able to walk dry-shod from point to point and it is necessary to be able to take the wheelbarrow from here to there and on to the rubbish heap in the corner, but paths have importance beyond this. They must add beauty to the garden, even if their presence makes mowing more time-taking.

The modern garden designers are showing us adventurous ways in which paths can be used, dismissing small tortuous geranium beds and transforming the rectangular plot into an amusing or at least satisfying pattern. There are hints to be taken from them—for it is the paths that make the lawn carpet interesting by widening, narrowing, bulging and dictating the shape of the lawn.

10 The Pool

Water is a perfect medium for a garden—ever changing, it gives movement and life.

Pools are more fashionable than ponds ever were, and are an attractive addition to town and country garden alike. They can be of concrete, plastic material or fibreglass, formal or informal in character and size, round, square, rectangular or kidney-shaped.

The construction of a pool should not be undertaken without the approval of a water engineer or the manufacturer of the particular pump unit to be used, while the local Electricity Board should be consulted and their approval sought regarding the electric installation, for unsuitable connections can be dangerous.

This is no place to discuss pumps but I would point out that in a small patio or on a terrace, silence in performance is important even if the quiet pump is more expensive than the noisy one.

The Concrete Pool

The owner having decided what depth of water the pool is to hold, excavation can begin.

The depth will depend on what the gardener wishes to grow. If the deep-growing Water-lilies are chosen, then special arrangements and deep sections must be provided for them so that their container may rest on the bottom of the pool.

Concrete walls on clay soil may require reinforced concrete of 4-6 ins. thickness, and must be allowed to harden thoroughly before the pool is filled.

A well-rammed, firm and level floor is essential if there is not to be uneven sinking, resulting in an inevitable leak.

Once a crack appears, it will be widened by the weight of the water and will have to be cut out down to a sound surface and re-packed with concrete—a considerable undertaking.

Prefabricated Pools

Pools of plastic material or glass-fibre are easy to establish. A hole is dug, the shell fitted, the lilies planted, the pool filled gradually with water and later the fish introduced.

A pool on a roof must be firmly packed round with well-rammed soil and shuttering to give it complete stability. If the roof cannot safely take more than fifty gallons of water, then a wall or gurgle fountain of some kind should be entertained.

The polythene-sheeting pool is made of the strongest gauge, known as 500. It is durable and, unless inadvertently punctured, should last for many years so long as the pool is kept filled with water. Trouble arises should the water level be allowed to fall, when the elements and in particular the sun undermine the strength of the exposed fabric.

The Rim

The formal concrete pool in a town garden is usually an artificial feature and a raised coping above lawn level suits it well.

A pool on a terrace should have a fairly substantial coping so that the visitor can beware.

The polythene-pool owner often masks the edge of the pool with marginal plants—Iris, Arum Lilies or Kingcups. There are pre-fabricated pools made with planting holes for this purpose, or gardeners can build in ledges at the edge of the water for their bog plants. Creeping subjects will also help in softening the line of demarcation between pool and lawn or paving.

It is welcome news that *Lobelia fulgens*, so often wrongly spoken of as *Lobelia cardinalis*, has been found to be happier grown as a bog plant in shallow water than as a border perennial, being hardier when its roots are covered by water. This lovely scarlet flower with deep claret foliage looks magnificent mirrored in the water.

The Water Hawthorn (*Aponogeton distachyus*) with scented white flowers and black stamens is one of the best deep marginals. But for the small pool, the Mimulus or Musk family and the well-known Water Forget-me-not are desirable moisture-loving companions.

Every pool has to be emptied from time to time when the water gets dirty or the plants become over-grown and in need of dividing.

The small pool can be bailed out or emptied by siphoning, but the large one will require a built-in drainage system and a soakaway.

Fountains

There are a number of small mechanical pumps to be had for working fountains and waterfalls that return the same water over and over again, while giving a pleasant rippling sound. There are jets that produce fan-shaped or plume sprays—or better still, a single dignified column of water.

There are also masks of lions, seals and porpoise-like mammals, and Greek heads all with water gushing from their mouths and handy basins to hang below them.

Small gurgle fountains that softly bubble, using pints rather than gallons of water have arrived at one of the large stores as I write, and have been snapped up for roof gardens.

Water-lilies

The Water-lily has pride of place in the water garden, and besides the beauty of the flowers there is the charm of the flat floating pads.

They can be grown in small pools, concrete tanks or tubs that hold water 6-12 ins. deep. Polythene crates are excellent for planting all aquatic plants, allowing plenty of freedom for root action.

March to July is the best planting time, when the water is warming up. Re-potting should be carried out every three years, using a rich turfy loam and a sprinkling of coarse bonemeal.

The Water-lily is a generous flowerer and must be well fed.

Varieties

When it comes to choosing plants, much will depend on the size and depth of the pool. The pads must be given the opportunity of floating. The large-flowered Water-lilies will usually be found the deepest growers.

Perhaps I should remind the beginner that should he wish to have fish in his pool, he must supply a depth of 18 ins., which necessitates the planting of the deeper-growing lilies.

It may well be that these will over-furnish a small pool and that he might, therefore, be wiser to keep his goldfish indoors in a bowl. An over-crowded pool with overlapping pads hiding the water's surface loses all interest and point.

When selecting varieties from a catalogue, 6-8 ins. must be allowed for the depth of soil in the planting crate.

The white Water-lily is surely the pick of the family and *odorata alba* or *minor* are ideal for the small pool.

'Gladstoniana' with large flowers and dominant yellow stamens needs plenty of room, while *pygmaea alba*, the smallest of the whites, has flowers no larger than a penny and succeeds in 2 or 3 inches of water.

Marliacea rosea will be found an easy medium-growing pink, but needs to establish itself before consenting to flower, while all members of the Laydekeri section in crimson, carmine and reddish shades are excellent for tubs and prefabricated containers.

'Sunrise' is the finest of the yellows but sometimes a hesitant grower, and soft yellow × *pygmaea helvola* is the perfect miniature.

When settled down and happy, Water-lilies flower from May to September.

Fish

Neither plants nor fish will prosper in a pool where there is a waterfall or forceful fountain and swirling movement.

Goldfish are more suitable for the small pool than swift and active Golden Orfe, always scouting near the surface for flies.

A fortnight or three weeks should be allowed to elapse between planting the Water-lilies and introducing the fish and Ramshorn snails. It is kind to feed the fish until they and the pool have settled down, but care must be taken not to give more food than is wanted, otherwise the left-overs will pollute the water.

Oxygenating and submerged plants are necessary to keep down algae, and the tangled vegetation is a pleasant shelter for the fish.

11 Trees

Choosing a tree is a serious matter; it is often the backbone of a town garden. Large trees are slow to grow and mature and for this reason should be planted by the young, but unfortunately the young are seldom gardeners, much less planters.

The townsman usually requires a tree as a single specimen. If he can make up his mind straightaway whether he wants an upright narrow fastigiate, weeping, or normal and ordinary shaped tree, deciduous or non-deciduous, it makes selection simpler.

Fastigiate Trees

The slim upright and fastigiate take up less space and suit the small garden where there is no ground to spare.

Betula alba fastigiata is an elegant fastigiate member of the **Birch** family, while *Carpinus betulus columnaris* (**Hornbeam**) is a useful pyramidal tree for those on heavy clay.

Crataegus monogyna stricta with erect branches is the fastigiate member of the **Thorn** family and a useful little tough.

Prunus erecta (alias *amanogawa*), the **Lombardy Poplar Cherry**, is the perfect vertical tree. The narrow column is a profusion of soft pink blossom in April and the leaves turn to a translucent yellow in the autumn. Pruning is seldom necessary and the cherries do not take kindly to the knife. In any case it is a pity to interfere with their natural bearing.

The **Oak's** representative is *Quercus pedunculata fastigiata*, pyramidal or broadly columnar in habit; the young growth of *Q. pedunculata* is a reddish-purple.

The **Robinia** (False Acacia), one of the most willing growers we have, contributes a columnar member *R. pseudoacacia pyramidalis* to end my abbreviated list. Exposed sites should be avoided as the tree's branches are brittle.

Perhaps I should warn the town gardener against the fast-growing **Lombardy Poplar** with its thirsty, far-seeking roots so often responsible for disturbing building foundations and drain-pipes. Even after the tree has been felled, the vigour of the suckers can be a nuisance.

Pendulous Trees

The weeper, unnatural in habit, is an acquired taste and anathema to some gardeners. I suppose I have inherited a sweet tooth for these plants as my father must have planted over fifty different pendulous species at my old home, Tittenhurst Park. The weeping *Cedrus atlantica glauca* planted over fifty years ago, known as the 'Ghost Trees', have become well-known garden personalities.

The pendulous tree is an excellent subject for a small garden, and *Prunus subhirtella pendula*, the **Weeping Spring Cherry**, with pale pink flowers that wreath its long slender branches, is one of the most beautiful of them.

The **Weeping Birch** and **Beech** look particularly well as specimen plants on a lawn, while the **Weeping Elm** that forms a flat-topped head with long pendulous branches makes a veritable umbrella.

The **Willow** (*Salix*) is one of the most graceful weepers we possess and it is untrue to say that it is merely a waterside plant, for there are some varieties that dislike damp conditions. In any case, it should not be planted at the water's edge, but at least a yard or two away.

The **Golden Weeping Willow**, *Salix chrysocoma* (*alba tristis*), (syn. *Vitellina pendula*), with slender branches of bright golden-yellow, is singularly attractive.

Tilia petiolaris (*argentea pendula*), the **Weeping Silver Lime**, with white richly-scented flowers, is another first-rate pendant tree.

Deciduous Trees

To avoid a tiresome catalogue list, I put forward in alphabetical order some of the trees that have pleased me the most.

The **Acers** or **Maples** are temperamental, but provided the soil is well-drained and a little shelter can be offered, they are worth a trial.

Acer brilliantissimum is, to my mind, the pick of the family, with suffused coral-pink spring foliage that gives, from a distance, the effect of a flowering shrub.

Acer palmatum is the popular member of the family that turns a striking red in the autumn.

Aesculus or **Horse-Chestnut**, including *A. carnea*, the red variety, is particularly delightful as a young tree, even if it outgrows the garden later on and has to be dismissed.

Ailanthus is the imposing Tree of Heaven, with a rounded head and greenish-white flowers that present themselves in terminal panicles. It is extremely tolerant of town conditions, in fact the bigger the city, the better it seems to grow, and its yellow autumn foliage attracts much attention in town squares and gardens.

The Tree of Heaven can be effectively pollarded if it should over-reach its allotted space.

Snowy Mespilus, the **Amelanchier**, deserves mention because of its tolerance. The profuse white flowers are followed by maroon-purple fruit.

The **Beech** (*Fagus*) has already been mentioned, but I must add a word about the **Ash** (*Fraxinus*). *Fraxinus ornus*, the Manna Ash, is the star of the family that gallantly stands up to wind, coastal conditions and smoke-polluted areas.

The **Birch** and **Hornbeam** have already been mentioned.

Now we come to a real favourite of mine that is a splendid Londoner—the **Catalpa** or Indian Bean. The golden variety, infinitely preferable to the green, is not always easy to come by.

The Golden Catalpa that I planted in Holland Park over twenty-five years ago is now some 25 ft. high—but I am still waiting for it to flower. I much regret that its trunk is not as straight as I would wish; it lost its stake support during the war years and never recovered its uprightness.

When buying this tree the gardener must press for *Catalpa aurea*: it is sometimes described in the catalogue as a slow grower that seldom makes a tree. Maybe I have been particularly lucky, but my experience encourages me to recommend the plant for London.

The **Judas Tree,** *Cercis siliquastrum*, is another favourite of mine, with rosy-lilac clusters of pea-shaped flowers that are borne on the joints of the branches and the main trunk in May.

This is a poor transplanter that must be bought young, and unfortunately it is only the mature that flower. But the Judas is one of the perfect trees for the small town garden and is worth the necessary patience.

There must be thousands of **Laburnums** in small town gardens. The tree has been tremendously popular over the last decade and has only lately begun to suffer from over-exposure.

L. × *vossii* with long racemes is the best garden form, while the amusing member of the genus is *L. adamii*, now known as Laburnocytisus, a graft hybrid between *Cytisus* (Broom) and Laburnum, resulting in possibly three different-coloured racemes appearing on the tree at the same time—yellow, purple and a mixture of the two.

The Laburnum rarely exceeds 20 ft. and is remarkably graceful. When children are about, it should be remembered that the tree's seeds are poisonous.

Liquidambar, the Sweet Gum, is grown for its wonderful crimson and gold autumn colour. This is a handsome, rather pyramidal tree that enjoys good loam and seldom succeeds on chalk.

The **Liriodendron** is the Tulip Tree with green-yellow cupped flowers; it often suffers a severe check after transplanting, but can be easily raised from seed by the patient.

The **Magnolia** is a member of a large genus of desirable plants both evergreen and deciduous which are best moved when the sap is rising and the plant just starting to make growth.

Among the deciduous, I recommend *M.* × *soulangeana*, with purple-tinged flowers, white within, that appear on leafless stems in April. A plant that has grown well for me in London.

M. lennei, with reddish-purple flowers deeper on the outside of the petals than within, is a beauty and *M. stellata*, the Star Magnolia, cannot be omitted for it is early, profuse and can be fitted into the smallest garden.

M. grandiflora is the much-loved evergreen with large glossy leaves and richly-scented cream flowers usually planted against a house or wall.

A plantsman will want to grow a species of interest and there can be few trees as interesting as the *Gingko biloba*, the **Maidenhair Tree**. I have recently seen a most beautiful specimen at Cannon

63

Hall, Hampstead, that must be one of the tallest in England. The fresh pale-green colour of its leaves is one of its charms.

The **Plane** (*Platanus*) is a familiar tree to the town dweller and the best tree for built-up areas, the peeling bark enabling the stem to free itself of soot and atmospheric pollution.

The **Prunus** genus is confusing to the novice, including as it does the Almond, Peach, Cherry, Plum, Apricot and others.

P. amygdalus pollardii is a good pronounced pink form of the **Common Almond** and the most popular member of the family. Unfortunately it is not a long-liver, but so desirable that it is worth growing for succession so that there is always a youngster to replace a fallen veteran.

The **Peach** (*P. persica*), slightly more tender than the Almond, will follow on in March and 'Clara Meyer' is bound to please.

Then there are the **Cherries,** unrivalled for their wealth of blossom, *amanogawa* and *subhirtella* have already been mentioned, but I must add *sargentii* with soft pink flowers and magnificently coloured foliage. The Bird Cherry (*P. padus*) has its admirers, and single-flowered *watereri* was deservedly given an Award of Garden Merit.

The generic names **Pyrus** and **Malus** are often confusing, since they include a number of unexpected species. The nursery-man's catalogue with a tangle of apples, whitebeams and pears often leads to further confusion. Clearly the crabs should have a place in this chapter as they provide fruit and colour not found in the cherry. 'John Downie' has charming white flowers and bright orange fruit that can be used for jelly-making, while 'Golden Hornet's' bright yellow, tapering fruit is always a temptation to the flower-arranger.

There are over three hundred members of the **Quercus** (Oak) genus. Its reputation as a slow grower is not altogether deserved, for if you treat a young sapling well, and above all leave it undisturbed, it soon makes headway. The quickest way of growing an oak may well be to start with an acorn.

Something has already been said about the *Robinia pseudoacacia* **Acacia** which has a tiresome habit of throwing up endless suckers, the **Lime** (*Tilia*) and **Elm** (*Ulmus*). Unfortunately the Dutch Elm disease is a serious threat to the Elm genus.

I end my deciduous tree list with a genus for the seaside gardener,

Gazebo and gravel courtyard patterned with Box
in a Knightsbridge garden, London

A pond and mock summer-house in Pelham Place, London,
once the home of Oliver Messel

the **Tamarix.** The pink flowers and feathery foliage of this maritime grower which, when happy, becomes more tree than shrub, reminds me of holidays spent at the seaside in my youth. Those who wish to be thus reminded should grow *T. pentandra*, which has delightful bright pink flowers in May.

Evergreen Trees

A well-shaped evergreen specimen gives character to a small garden; the unclipped have, as a rule, more distinction than those under the knife. A handsome conifer, a Holly, an Ilex—even if it does shed its leaves heedlessly—are trees to treasure.

Some gardeners will have inherited a *Cedrus atlantica glauca*, an Edwardian favourite that followed those popular Victorians, the Monkey-Puzzle and Wellingtonia, occupying as if by right the centre bed of the front garden.

But these are giants, and it is the dwarfs and the low-growing that are wanted for the town.

The gardener looking for a small conifer might consider one of the following: *Abies hudsonia*, a pigmy from White Mountains of New Hampshire, growing to only 1-2 ft.

Cedrus libani nana, a slow-growing, dense miniature cedar.

Cryptomeria japonica cristata, with amusing cockscomb growth.

Juniperus communis compressa, a bluish-grey alpine columnar conifer rarely exceeding 2 ft. The remarkable dwarf *Libocedrus decurrens* var. *intricata* with flat and twisted branchlets that seems to mark time will suit the miniature garden.

These are but a few of an army of curiosities that will delight the plantsman.

But it has to be faced that conifers as a whole do not like town life, which is the reason they are so seldom seen in industrial areas. It is often difficult to keep them going.

Pot and tub specimens are likely to be more successful as they can be moved and kept clean by regular washing.

Tree Care

All newly-planted trees should be staked, and staked with care, so that there is no chafing through ties being too loose nor discomfort through being too tight.

The stake should be driven down two feet, preferably before planting, so that it is firm enough to resist the swing and rock of the tree.

Any branch or roots damaged in transplanting should be removed, making a smooth vertical cut and then painting the wound with Arbrex, white lead paint or a reputable wound-healer. Any wound at any time of more than half an inch in diameter should be treated in this manner.

Young trees must not be allowed to go dry in spring or summer and no turf or weeds should be permitted to grow at their base for two years or more.

Care of Large Trees

The gardener has a number of duties to the public and one of the most important of these is to see that his trees are safe.

If a tree is dying back and there are signs of rot, peeling or fungus, these must be regarded as danger signals, particularly in the case of large elms. Heavy branches that fall without warning are a considerable risk.

The Parks Department of the local authority concerned is usually willing to inspect trees and to advise on their treatment, and a good-looking tree should not be felled until the specialist has said it must come down.

A forester in Windsor Park once told me that he liked to watch the veteran oaks in a gale, because he could then see by their give, take and sway their state of health and foreseeable length of life.

Instant Trees

Not everybody will be able to afford the luxury of a ready-made tree, although if there is money to spare, the beauty and shade is a good investment. The transplanting method of the experts in moving these giant trees will be informative and helpful in principle to gardeners moving small saplings and shrubs, which is my reason for giving it here.

Instant trees, usually referred to by the landscape architect as 'semi-mature' or 'extra-heavy standard trees', are from 20-35 ft. in height and from twenty to fifty years of age. They cost anything from £50 to £200. The extra-heavy standard tree is nursery-grown and usually sold when from 15-20 ft. in height; these cost approximately £1 per foot of their height. Examples of semi-mature trees can be seen in the planting of Norway Maples at Marble Arch, which come from Exbury Gardens, Southampton, and there are extra-heavy standards in a row in Kingsway which were planted in 1964. Exbury has led the way with this new tree-planting method and any order placed for a 15-20 ft. standard in the spring is delivered on the client's doorstep in the autumn.

It is interesting to see these splendid young saplings grown and prepared for this method of transplanting. As at all nurseries which have the necessary man-power, plants are moved once or twice while young in order to produce a compact fibrous rootball and so avoid large tap roots growing too deep into the ground. Fibrous root action is encouraged by planting in a mixture of light loam and peat. When it comes to lifting, the rootball is carefully wrapped in sacking so that the soil does not fall away during transport.

To prepare the larger semi-mature trees for moving is a more complicated matter. A trench is cut, circling the rootball approximately 2½ ft. from the centre stem, and the protruding roots are severed from the plant. The trench is then filled with a mixture of loam and peat to encourage the formation of fibrous roots. During a summer drought the tree must be regularly and generously watered. It is then usually left in place for two years, after which it can easily be lifted and moved to its new location.

Preparation for planting is done in varying ways, but Exbury recommends that the base of the prepared hole should be lined with old turf and the rootball well anchored to prevent any movement. The planting of these semi-mature trees can be done during any of the winter months, but frosty conditions should be avoided and if the trees are transplanted during a dry spell they must be copiously watered in and mulched.

The tree's leaf formation in the first season after planting may not be luxuriant, but the second year should see it in full leaf. If drought should persist during the first summer season, care must be taken that the tree is not allowed to dry out.

12 Shrubs

Most of us begin our gardening career with a love of flowers and we plant herbaceous borders and rose-beds galore. We buy bedding plants in the late spring that will give us a gay return a few weeks later.

But if we live to become mature gardeners then we cease to ask for a quick return and look for plants that are more enduring, that will improve year by year and respond according to our skill. After all, there is only one excuse for growing those soup-plate Dahlias (for no one can call them beautiful): the fact that they are mighty difficult.

So the mature gardener inevitably becomes a shrub man. In his salad days he will be tempted to plant trees and shrubs that would soon grow too large for their positions. It seems almost impossible to resist being allured in this way.

Perhaps I should remind the novice that the bed against the house is usually specially favoured, being not only protected against frost but often benefiting from the warmth of the house, and therefore should be allocated to those for whom he has a particular regard.

I now give a by no means exhaustive list of the deciduous and evergreen shrubs that will stand up to town life.

Deciduous Shrubs

The deciduous **Azalea**, a member of the rhododendron family, has come a long way during the last decade. The Ghent and the *mollis* groups have not been entirely superseded, but the Exbury and Knap Hill hybrids are clearly preferred by most gardeners and are an improvement on those that have gone before.

A number of these hybrids have the Royal Horticultural Society's Award of Merit, which guarantees their performance. The Exbury strain has a specially attractive colour-range, many varieties being beautifully blotched, and specialist nurserymen offer plants propagated vegetatively and by seed from the late Mr Lionel de Rothschild's collection.

I am delighted to hear that veteran yellow sweet-scented *Azalea pontica* (syn. *rhododendron luteum*), looked upon by some as wanting in breeding, is still much appreciated by the gardening public. It is a grand plant and it is cheap.

Azaleas and Rhododendrons should have their blooms removed when faded, but care must be taken not to damage the new buds growing immediately below them.

Buddleia davidi showed us what a willing town grower it can be both during and after the war when it threw up its long purple plumes that invite the butterflies.

This is a plant for quick effect now to be had in all shades from mauve to darkest purple and pink, while there are white varieties with graceful heads of bloom. These plants require to be cut back fearlessly in February, removing all but 2 ins. of the wood made the previous year.

B. alternifolia is the distinguished member of the family that should be treated as a specimen plant. Its willow-like foliage and rose-mauve June flowers cascade like a waterfall.

B. globosa is robust and more pedestrian, with globular yellow-tangerine flowers.

B. davidi nanhoensis is an elegant mauve-flowered dwarf.

Ceanothus is always admired, but alas, this plant is tender and even if given a wall for protection, established plants get caught and killed by the frost year by year, which is cruelly disappointing. The hardiest variety is probably sky-blue 'Gloire de Versailles'.

Ceratostigma is a hardy Plumbago with charming blue flowers and red-tinted autumn foliage. *C. willmottianum* is a good mixer, either in front of shrubs or in the plant border, and gains in charm if mass-planted.

Chaenomeles, syn. Cydonia, syn. Japonica, the Flowering Quince, has the ability to grow almost anywhere. C. 'Knap Hill Scarlet' has made a great name, but I prefer the quieter apple-blossom *moerloesii* and pure white *nivalis* has charm.

Chimonanthus praecox (syn. **fragrans**), **Winter Sweet,** is not an easy town plant, often taking years to establish itself, but as I have known gardeners succeed in getting the plant to flower in London, I feel its wonderfully fragrant yellow sprays deserve mention.

Clerodendron trichotomum (the Glory Tree) will enjoy a sunny, well-drained position and give white star-like flowers in summer, followed by surprising china-blue berries with crimson calyces.

It is difficult to speak too highly of the **Cornus** or **Dogwood** family. *Cornus kousa chinensis*, with creamy-white bracts borne on wide spreading branches in June, is superb, and *C. mas*, the Cornelian Cherry, with small yellow flowers followed by red fruits in January, is in its way equally beautiful.

The **Cotoneaster** is a large genus including evergreen as well as deciduous species. *C. frigida*, introduced in 1824, should be better known for its striking scarlet fruits, but it is *C. horizontalis*, the Fish-bone, that has had the publicity, this being an excellent wall, rockery or bank plant, lying flat on the ground, with sparkling white May flowers followed by orange-red berries.

Something has already been said about the **Crataegus** (Hawthorn) in pink, scarlet and white, usually at their best in June rather than in May, and prepared to grow in any soil on almost any site.

Cytisus (Broom) glories in the sun and a light soil, but the plants are apt to get shabby in town, where they are seldom long-lived.

The fragrant **Daphne mezereum** and the dwarf *D. cneorum* are most desirable, if a little temperamental.

The hybrid **Deutzias** are splendid June flowerers and there are a number of good white and pink-mauve varieties. They, and the Diervilla (known until recently as Weigela), are excellent town shrubs that respond to manuring and mulching. *D. venusta variegata*, with golden-edged foliage and rose-pink flowers, is extremely decorative.

Euonymus, Forsythia and **Fuchsia** have already been mentioned, so now to the **Halesia,** or Snowdrop Tree, with spreading branches hung with pendulous white flowers in May. It should be noted that it is a lime-hater.

Hamamelis (Witch Hazel), one of the most attractive of winter-flowering shrubs and another lime-hater, seems indifferent to a smoky atmosphere but is often slow to settle down and flower. Its yellow-ribbon-like flowers and delicious scent make it worth a trial.

Gardening friends of mine assure me they have done well with **Hibiscus syriacus coeleste** and **rubis**. Handsome single and double-flowered varieties will be found in the nurseryman's catalogue for those who wish to try their hand. The single-flowered varieties will be found the more co-operative.

Every reader will be familiar with the **Hydrangea** and here the gardener has a wide choice.

I love the lacecaps and in particular *macrophyla* 'Blue Wave', with central florets of purplish-blue when on lime-free soil.

However, the *hortensis* types seen in the florists' shops, with huge heads of blooms (red or pink, limey-blue when in acid soils), are preferred by many. Blueing powder is to be had from Boots the Chemist or the sundriesman.

Whatever the choice, *H. paniculata grandiflora* must be considered, for with its huge tapering panicles of creamy-white flowers which fade pink, it is a delight.

Few of the hydrangeas can claim complete hardiness; in cold areas they should be given straw or bracken protection and dead blooms should be left on until severe frosts are over.

Philadelphus, better known as Syringa (the right name for Lilac and hence the common confusion), has one of the loveliest of all scents. It loves the sun and a feed of manure and is too often denied both. The gardener should have a care that he is not sold one of the new large-flowered varieties that are sadly unscented.

Rhus (Sumach) is the perfect shrub for the townsman, possessing the most beautiful and brilliant autumn foliage.

R. typhina, the Stag's Horn Sumach, is my pick. It grows into a small, flat-topped 'tree' of 8-10 ft., often forking from the base; the pinnate leaves, 1-2 ft. long, turn to bright orange and red in the autumn.

Ribes or Flowering Currant in shades of pink and crimson has a scent that may displease. *R. sanguineum* 'Pulborough Scarlet' is a deep red and an improvement on former varieties.

Rosemary is a woody fragrant shrub and not always a willing town grower, preferring light soil and a more southern climate. *R. officinalis* is the old 'Rosemary for remembrance'. R. × *pyramidalis*, ('Jessop's Upright'), is an erect form with spire-like stems.

The common form should be trimmed after flowering and again in April if necessary and not allowed to sprawl. Erectus and Jessop's, being tidy growers, do not require the knife.

Roses have been given a chapter to themselves.

Sambucus (Elder) can be valuable in industrial districts but looks a trifle coarse in distinguished company. However, *S. nigra* 'aurea', the Golden Elder, can be kept in place by regular spring pruning. The Red Elder, *S. racemosa* and *S. r. plumosa aurea*, a slow grower with finely-cut foliage, also deserves a mention.

Spiraea is another useful family, provided the gardener chooses his varieties with care. *S. × arguta* 'Bridal Wreath', festooned in white, is a splendid shrub and incidentally makes a lovely hedge. *S. × bumalda* 'A. Waterer' is crimson and excellent for the front of the border.

Syringa, often spoken of as Lilac, survives rather than grows in many a town garden, but alas at its worst—starved and antiquated, some of the bushes having been planted over twenty-five years ago. These washed-out mauve varieties have been surpassed in form and size without loss of scent.

It has to be admitted that modern hybridization has spoiled, even ruined, some flowers altogether by making them too coarse and opulent, but this is not the case with such beauties as double white Lilac 'Madame Lemoine', crimson 'Souvenir de Louis Spath', soft pink 'Buffon', and a host of other twentieth-century introductions.

I know of only one lilac garden and that is in Suffolk, but it may be the idea will appeal to a townsman looking for a hobby plant. There is a long list of pink, purple, carmine, red, white, cream and yellow double and single varieties, bushes or standards to choose from, as well as the plume-like Canadian hybrids and a number of tall-growing species of distinction and interest.

The flowering period on average would be early to mid-May; mid to late May, and early June. A short season perhaps, but weeks of beauty and astonishing scent.

May I remind lilac owners that they should remove the flower-heads as soon as they fade and spare the plant's energy.

Evergreen Shrubs

Many of us live to be middle-aged before we begin to appreciate the evergreens. There must be something a little melancholy about them to make us feel this way—a churchyard association, or our subconscious remembers the gloomy drip of the shrubbery when playing hide-and-seek in our youth.

But the time surely comes when we recognize that it is the evergreens—the Arbutus, the Yews, the Hollies, Camellias, Rhododendrons and other handsome shrubs—that make the English gardens what they are.

Arbutus (the Strawberry Tree) bears delightful pink or white flowers and small strawberry-like fruits simultaneously.

A. unedo, with creamy pitcher-shaped flowers, is a lovely evergreen shrub for the small garden, provided it is not on lime or in a cold part of the country. This is an aristocrat that needs a suitable position.

The evergreen **Berberis,** with yellow flowers in the spring and violet berries in the winter, is a plant of character. Some of the most suitable members of the genus have been assigned to the Mahonia family. (See page 76.)

Buxus (Box) can be used for amusing clipped topiary specimens. The gardener would be wise to try his hand at balls and pyramids before attempting bears and peacocks.

We now know that the **Camellia** is as hardy as the Laurel, but the flower-buds are vulnerable to early-morning sun after frost, particularly when wet with rain. They are also sensitive to cold north and east winds and are really happiest on a south-west wall.

Camellias are peat-lovers and dislike lime or chalk soils: they should be found a partially shaded position.

'Donation's' clear pink semi-double flowers that turn to deep peach, and 'J. C. Williams's' pale blush blooms with prominent yellow stamens are exquisite.

The evergreen **Ceanothus** is safest on a warm south wall, for it is not completely hardy. *C. dentatus* is a good early flowerer and *C. × burkwoodii*, with bright blue summer to autumn flowers, is rightly immensely popular.

73

The sweet-scented **Choisya** likes a mild climate but I have seen it flowering profusely in a North London garden. It requires a dry situation and light soil, and is tolerant of partial shade.

Cistus (Rock-rose) is only looked upon as hardy by the optimist. When we get a severe winter there is invariably a high mortality rate among the genus. However, they strike easily from cuttings and a few plants given extra protection can be used for propagation.

This is the perfect plant for a dry sunny bank. It should be shaped by pinching out the tips of the young shoots and not heavily pruned.

C. laurifolius withstood the frosts of 1963 and is probably the hardiest member of the family, but those in a warm corner of the country might like to try *C.* × 'Silver Pink', a delicate pink semi-dwarf with silvery foliage.

The **Cotoneaster** (of which the deciduous varieties have already been mentioned) is a splendidly berried shrub. *C. franchetii* has graceful greyish foliage, orange-scarlet berries and a spreading habit, while *C. microphylla*, with prostrate and pendulous growth and bright red berries, is a true evergreen that accommodates itself willingly against a low wall.

The deciduous **Daphne** has already been mentioned, but I recommend evergreen *D. cneorum*, rose-pink and sweet-scented, tender and difficult, to any plantsman looking for a real challenge.

There are twenty or more members of the **Elaeagnus** (Wood Olive) family. But the striking variety is *pungens aureo-variegata*, with prominent central leaf variegation of golden-yellow. This shrub is hardy, and equally happy in the border, tub or window-box, in the town or at the seaside, and is a help in brightening up a dull planting.

E. × *ebbingei* has silver-green foliage and small silvery-white flowers.

Erica (Heath) is a special taste and several Hampstead enthusiasts are proud of growing a large number of species and exciting plantings that give an all-the-year-round effect.

The *carnea*, × *darleyensis* and *mediterranea* groups are more tolerant of lime than most. Of the carneas, carmine 'King George', 'Springwood Pink' or 'Springwood White' are bound to please and will flower through the winter and spring. No heather-lover should

74

be without *E. vagans* 'Mrs Maxwell', the wonderful cerise Cornish Heath in flower from July to October, and the long sprays of double pink *Calluna* 'H. E. Beale'.

Having already said something about the **Escallonia** and **Euonymus,** I come to the Tassel Bush, the distinctive **Garrya elliptica,** which, when laden with catkins in winter, must be one of the most decorative wall shrubs we possess. The female plant has a different charm: long clusters of black fruits.

The **Hebe** (alias Veronica) is another large genus that is very ornamental in the spring and may be planted in town or seaside, provided the climate is mild.

H. brachysiphon (syn. *traversii*) 'White Gem' is popular, and 'Autumn Glory,' an intense violet-blue, will flower continuously from June until October. The unopened buds have a silver tint and the foliage is shaded purple.

H. hulkeana is the belle of the family, but is tender and should be attempted only by those in the south who have a warm corner to offer.

The **Hypericum,** Rose of Sharon or St John's Wort family, claims hardy and half-hardy shrubs and herbaceous perennials, but here I mention one evergreen only, *H. patulum* 'Hidcote', the finest of them all, with saucer-like flowers of shining yellow that come from July to October. This fine shrub grows to 3-4 ft. and is extraordinarily easy to please, given a spot of sunshine.

The **Ilex,** or Holly, needs no recommendation from me. 'Golden King', a berrying form, 'Golden Queen' and 'Silver Queen', both non-berrying, are splendid evergreens. Hollies are dioecious, which means that females must be chosen if berries are wanted, and a few males must be planted in the offing to pollinate them.

The **Kalmia** (Calico Bush), with flat clusters of pink flowers and glossy leaves, is a desirable plant for those on lime-free soil. Its beauty justifies its trial.

Laurus (Sweet Bay) is a little tender but does well in coastal areas. Its aromatic leaves will be appreciated by an enlightened cook.

Lavender, greatly valued for its fragrance, succeeds whole-heartedly only in light and well-drained soils where it get the sunshine. An immediate trim after flowering will keep this old-world plant from becoming a straggler.

Mahonia japonica, until recently known as *Berberis bealei* is impossible to fault. It is a Japanese species, with pinnate leaves and lovely winter clusters of pendulous racemes of lemon-yellow flowers that have a delicious lily-of-the-valley scent. It enjoys partial shade and good ordinary soil.

Myrtus, the common Myrtle, is a delightfully fragrant bush but is for mild districts only.

Olearia is the white Daisy Bush. *O. haastii* flowers profusely from July onwards and stands up nobly to smoky industrial areas. Flowers should be removed as they fade, otherwise they stay on and give the plant a depressing look.

Osmanthus, with white fragrant April flowers and small dark green leaves, deserves to be better known. *O. delavayi,* thriving in any soil in mild districts, was given an Award of Garden Merit as long ago as 1923.

Pernettya, with berries in white, pink, lilac and red, is a showy dwarf shrub for lime-free soil. *P. mucronata,* with wiry stems and white heather-like flowers, berries persistently if male and female plants are present (one male to five to seven females).

Gardeners on acid peaty soil will want to grow the **Pieris** with its May-blooming, creamy-white, lily-of-the-valley-like flowers. This is a very ornamental shrub requiring much the same fare as the Rhododendron.

P. formosa forrestii has brilliant scarlet young shoots that stand out against the mature deep green foliage and from a distance are often mistaken for blossom. The Pieris is an arresting plant that should have a place out of the sun near the doorway of a house where it is constantly on view. It is a slow grower that seldom trespasses.

Now we come to an important, large and diverse genus, the **Rhododendron.** Perhaps I should begin with the aristocrats—the species. These early flowerers can be exacting but, cosseted with mulches of leaf-mould, I have seen them in very good order together with Camellias in gardens both in Kensington and St John's Wood. *R. augustinii,* with rather small pale blue-purple flowers, superb in the early spring, is a delight.

All the species should come from a reliable source. There are *augustiniis* and *augustiniiis*—and their performance will depend on where you buy them. Reliable firms propagate from the best forms

76

of the plant only and therefore it is wise to buy from a specialist with a renowned collection.

A good species Rhododendron is a valuable acquisition to any garden and often an expensive one. The plant should therefore be carefully sited with evergreen shelter and planted if possible where it will be seen from the house. The usual flowering time for the species is April or May, when it may be too cold to stand out-doors and admire for as long as one would wish.

The following species have great distinction and should be con-sidered by a plantsman looking for an outstanding specimen plant. Yellow *campylocarpum*, red *cinnabarinum*, pale-yellow *wightii* and shell-pink *williamsianum* are all unusual and exciting subjects.

The Chinese and other Asiatic hybrids have a contribution to make to the town garden. Among them violet 'Bluebird', perfect for the front of a border, with lavender 'Blue Diamond' and 'Blue Tit' somewhere in the background. Or perhaps low-spreading 'Elizabeth', with its lovely dark-red trumpet flowers, alongside neat and tidy yellow 'Hawk'. Meanwhile, lilac-pink 'Naomi' may suit those who prefer the gentler shades.

So much for the stars of the genus and I now turn to the more commonplace but indispensable hybrids. These are for general planting, flowering generously in late May or early June. Peat, leaf-mould and filtered sunlight are all they ask.

Gardeners who do not know pink 'Christmas Cheer' should make its acquaintance because it is one of the few Rhododendrons that bursts into bloom in February or even earlier in warm localities. It is a delightful surprise turn.

The following hardy hybrids are a selection from a large group, flowering in late May and early June.

'Cynthia', the veteran and much-seen rose-crimson bedder that can always be relied upon (other than when on lime); 'Loder's White'; 'Mrs G. W. Leak', pink with a brown-purple blotch, my pick of the hardy hybrids; 'Pink Pearl', the most popular variety ever raised; lovely 'Purple Splendour'; and 'Susan', a lavender with deeper markings.

Now for yet another group of the Rhododendron genus—the Azalea, smaller but as beautiful as any of the clan. The tall-growing are deciduous and have already been dealt with; the low-growing are evergreen.

A. mucronatum (semi-deciduous) should not be missed: it is one of the most popular white evergreen azaleas, but it is to the Japanese dwarf Kurume varieties that the gardener should turn, for they are low and spreading and, growing to about 2-3 ft., are excellent for the small garden. There is an avalanche of beautiful varieties but I must mention at least two of them—clear pink 'Hinomayo' and pure white 'Palestrina'. They are a superb couple on which to close my note on the Rhododendron clan.

Skimmia is a compact bush—the female plant carrying bright red winter berries. *S. japonica* is useful, growing happily on lime or acid soils in semi-shade. The white flowers are fragrant.

Veronica—*see under* Hebe.

Having already emphasized the beauty of **Viburnum tinus,** the well-known winter-flowering Laurustinus, I come lastly to the **Yucca,** about whose texture and form Gertrude Jekyll has been so magnanimous.

I had a personal dislike for the Yucca in my youth and have only lately accepted and appreciated its true value.

The Yucca is the Adam's Needle, flowering from July to September. *Y. filamentosa*, growing to 4-5 ft., throws up amazing spikes of cream-white flowers that might have come straight from the tropics. However, it is splendidly hardy and, oddly enough, a member of the Lily family.

Shrub Protection

Winds can be destructive to the tender and it is generally the east and north winds that are the problem.

The newly-planted are vulnerable and even the hardy subjects, when young, may need protection in an exposed garden.

Screens are dealt with elsewhere, but beyond the shelter of walls, screens, wattle hurdles and the communal windbreaks, individual protection should be given to the specially tender or treasured.

A solid branch of fir firmly stuck into the ground on the windward side of a plant will help to break the force of the wind. The wind-barrier should be erected fairly close to the plant but it is important that there should be at least an 18-in. gap between the protective screen and the plant. Frozen matting or material pressed against branches is a danger.

A cone-shaped wigwam or tent affair is the best method of protecting the very tender so long as the wind can filter through it. If too solid, the defeated blast may well eddy round the structure, creating a small whirlpool, and lift it away.

Whatever the design, the barrier must be secured to stakes, or better still, to a wooden frame.

Bracken or straw pressed between two sheets of netting makes a successful barrier and can be shaped into a cylindrical pattern. It should be a little taller than the plant and I cannot over-stress the importance of never entirely enclosing the plant. If the structure is slightly open-ended, the gardener can add a little extra straw or bracken packing around his plant if he thinks it necessary.

At the end of April the wigwam can go.

Transplanting

Deciduous trees and shrubs are best moved from October to March. But if bad weather prevails throughout January and February, transplanting can be delayed until March.

Evergreens are best planted in September or late March or early April when root growth is active.

13 Hedges

A hedge is usually a long-term investment, so a careful choice of plants should be made. The size of the garden and the purpose of the hedge are first considerations.

Is it to be a windbreak, a screen, a barrier or a boundary, or an ornamental hedge just to look pretty? Is it to be formal or informal?

An 8 or 9 ft. hedge will filter the wind on the terrace, and Beech, Hornbeam and Yew make delightful windbreaks if the garden is big enough. The Hornbeam will be found to do better than the Beech on clay and wet soil.

Yew has an undeservedly poor reputation for slow growth, but given good soil when planted and regularly watered in dry weather, it will settle down in its second year and grow 10-12 ins. a year. Gardeners in a hurry may care to lay pipes down to the roots of the plants for watering to ensure that they never go dry. I have seen a hedge cosseted in this way materialize in double-quick time.

Beech is a favourite of mine, making a dense screen and keeping its russet leaves right through the winter. It is greatly enhanced if a Copper Beech is added here and there. The mixed hedge of these two Beeches can be as attractive as the tapestry hedge made up of a number of subjects.

The easily-pleased **Laurel** and **Privet** are too often scorned. The thick laurel leaf should be trimmed with secateurs rather than shears, for a series of leaves cut in half is a deplorable sight. The Portugal Laurel also deserves a mention; it is tough and can be either kept low or left to grow to 6 ft. or more.

Privet is looked down upon because it is seldom seen at its best. That it lives at all in some of the unfavourable conditions it has to face is to its credit.

Like its more distinguished fellows, it benefits from an occasional

Lilium regale growing in a St Marylebone area

Tulipa princeps, a pool and reflected Narcissi in a London garden

mulch of compost, grass mowings (only half an inch thick), leaf-mould, or spent hops in the spring after a downpour of rain. This mulch will help to conserve moisture through the summer. Weeds must be controlled and the hedge should be given a thorough over-haul, removing all debris in the late autumn and again in the spring.

It clips well and when in good heart should be tipped three or four times a year.

Nine broad-leaved Green to one of Golden Privet, when well-cared for, will make a most attractive hedge. If the town con-ditions are favourable, a Quickthorn may be added here and there to give the hedge a solid and more resistant quality. I ask gardeners to be more generous in every way to the Privet. Oh, its greed im-poverishes its neighbours—but what of that?

Conifers

There is a big demand for plants and hedges that will quickly shut out a neighbour's house or an eyesore of some kind.

Cupressocyparis × *leylandii* is one answer. It is a columnar tree with spraying grey-green foliage and it is a lightning grower. Some gardeners have trouble in trimming this plant into a hedge because of its height and the lack of a tall enough ladder. It does well by the sea and seems heedless of the wind.

Chamaecyparis lawsoniana makes a rich green hedge for those who want a tall screen and are willing to let the plants grow their own way without interference. Its feathery growth may lose its good appearance if carelessly trimmed, but it is a great stand-by. *Chamaecyparis* 'Green Hedger', raised by Jackman's of Woking, makes a good dense hedge and deserves consideration.

Cupressus macrocarpa from California has not been able to accli-matize itself fully to our climate and, having disappointed many gardeners, cannot be recommended as a long-liver.

Flowering and Berried Hedges

We must be grateful to the **Aucuba** or Spotted Laurel, for it will grow in almost any soil in full sun, dense shade, or the dank or airless corner. It should be grown in clumps if berries are expected, with perhaps one male to six or more female-flowered plants.

Aucuba japonica is the green-leaved male form and *A. variegata* (syn. *maculata*) the variegated female form.

The majority of the **Berberis** family manage to thrive in almost any soil, stand up well to clipping and make an impenetrable hedge. *B.* × *stenophylla* gives a delightful performance of yellow flowers on arching stems in April and May. *B. darwinii* is also outstanding and the orange flowers are followed by round blue berries; both these are evergreen.

Cotoneaster lactea, an olive-green evergreen that has white flowers and bunches of orange-red fruits, and **Pyracantha rogersiana,** with white flowers and red berries, can both be relied upon to make grand hedges if given enough light and air.

Escallonia is a sea-lover that succeeds in certain mild areas, and 'Slieve Donard' with large apple-blossom flowers is a hardy variety. Shiny-leaved plants such as this will normally grow in towns and survive all but the deepest shade.

Euonymus europaeus, the Spindle Tree, with rose-coloured capsules and orange-red seeds, is useful in a town garden, while *E. japonica* is probably the best for the seaside. The flowers are unimportant but the bright berries are a compensation.

Hebe (alias **Veronica**) **anomala,** with white star flowers, will succeed in towns in the south along with the Daisy Bush, *Olearia haastii*, the Myrtle, and the flower arrangers' treasured Pittosporum.

Holly is a dense evergreen, very splendid when decorated with red berries, but a dust collector and sometimes a bad starter. *Ilex aquifolium camelliaefolia*, a good form with smooth-edged leaves, is quite a happy town dweller.

Lonicera nitida, fertilis, an improvement on *L. nitida,* the Shrubby Honeysuckle, has slightly larger leaves and plenty of fruit, but I doubt whether it is a long-liver.

Prunus myrobalana, not unlike the Blackthorn, and **Cerasifera nigra** (alias **pissardii**), the well-known purple-foliaged plant with blush-pink flowers, make a striking hedge; they can be used effectively if planted alternately.

I wish we had **Syringa** (Lilac) hedging in the fields in this country as they do in Denmark. *Syringa* × *chinensis saugeana* (*rubra*) stands up to the knife if trimmed after its lovely purple flowers have faded and makes quite a dense hedge. *Syringa vulgaris* hybrids spaced at $1\frac{1}{2}$ ft. intervals will also give a good display.

Tamarix, a maritime genus with feathery flowers and foliage, is bravely resistant to the wind. The silvery-leaved Sea Buckthorn, with lanceolate silvery leaves and masses of orange berries, is a striking shrub for seaside gardeners.

Viburnum tinus is the ever-useful Laurustinus, the well-known pink-and-white winter flowerer.

The Informal Hedge

If your soil is lime-free there is no better informal boundary plant than the **Rhododendron** or **Azalea.**

They are free flowerers and they keep well furnished at their bases.

The Rhododendron has become a specialist's plant and if you wish for a distinguished species or cross such as a yellow 'Crest' seedling, you will find it only at Exbury Gardens, near Southampton.

Here is an opportunity for the plantsman to grow something a little unusual if conditions are favourable, and I remind him of the beautiful hedge of *R.* × *praecox* at the Royal Botanical Gardens, Edinburgh.

R. × *praecox*, bushy and low-growing, has delightful pink-mauve flowers and is among the earliest spring performers. I am not dreaming when I say I have seen it covered in bloom in St John's Wood, London.

The hardy hybrids will no doubt be the usual choice, being bright, easy and comparatively cheap. 'Purple Splendour' with black markings and 'Loder's White' are two of the best, and 'Pink Pearl' will, it seems, go on for ever.

R. ponticum, unfortunately looked upon as common, is rarely appreciated and *Azalea pontica*, yellow and sweetly scented, is also spoken of in a condescending way. Both these are useful plants and the Azalea quite lovely.

Others to be considered for a low hedge are the **Forsythia,** and here I prefer the veteran pale yellow *suspensa* varieties to the newer brash golden *spectabilis*; the **Ribes** or Flowering Currant in palest pink to dark crimsons that look well when interplanted; and, in a warm part of the country in a sheltered place, the red and purple **Fuchsia magellanica** var. **riccartonii** is happy and floriferous.

83

Low-Growing and Dwarf Hedges

Box is quite a good town shrub if trimmed in spring and summer and well fed.

Heather-lovers might like to try some of the Ericas and Callunas, choosing those tolerant of alkaline soil if on lime, and treating them to plenty of peat.

The **Potentilla,** with white-yellow and tangerine flowers that have a long period of bloom, can be pruned to form quite a satisfactory hedge.

Santolina, with woolly foliage and a silvery gloss, like Lavender, Rosemary and other silver-foliage plants, does not care for town life; these are best grown as single plants. Otherwise, the gardener is saddled with a hedge requiring constant repair.

The Rose Hedge

The Rose makes a superb hedge, provided a suitable type is chosen.

One of the most beautiful hedges I have seen was in Suffolk not far from Ipswich: it was of *R. xanthina spontanea*, known familiarly as Canary Bird, and I have also seen a decorative hedge of *R. moyesii*, with single intense crimson-red blooms with a circle of cream stamens that are followed in the autumn by flagon-shaped hips. These are hedges of great floral beauty but I am a little doubtful whether they are going to be long-lived. The sturdy Wichuraiana 'Albertine', much loved, sweet-scented, copper-pink, would be a better choice in an exposed position.

The summer-flowering Penzance hybrid Sweet Briars make a splendid tall hedge from 5-8 ft., depending on their variety and the skill of the pruner. I have to admit the group is vulnerable to black spot, but this disease is usually less troublesome in industrial or town areas.

Many of the floribundas and hybrid musks will make satisfactory medium-height hedges.

'Queen Elizabeth', the first grandiflora, a glorious clear pink, upright, vigorous, free-flowering with plenty of foliage, must surely be the best hedge plant we have. Very often tiresomely tall in a bed, it is ideal as a five-foot boundary plant. Deep crimson 'Frensham', with the strong growth desirable for low hedges, is unfortunately too prone to mildew to be recommended.

Most of the climbers and ramblers can be trained on suitable supports to which the roses can be tied in as soon as they make enough growth. They should be pruned hard to about a foot from the ground so that they make plenty of sturdy basal growth, but not until established. The perpetual flowerers such as 'Pink Perpétue', 'Golden Showers', and 'Danse du Feu' are a valuable addition to the garden.

'Zéphirine Drouhin', the pink semi-climbing thornless rose, is not a true perpetual but deserves a place in every garden. It can be led upwards to some 5-6 ft. if treated lightly with the knife.

Now that the old-fashioned and once neglected roses are to the fore again, there are roses and roses for everybody.

Buying and Planting

Hedging plants can be bought by the dozen and small plants of about 2 ft. make the best hedges, establishing themselves without check. Growing fast, they soon catch up with the larger plants of the same species transplanted at the same time.

Planting is better done in the autumn, but can be left until the early spring so long as the plants are installed before budburst.

A trench 3 ft. wide and at least 2 ft. deep should be prepared, the bottom of the trench broken up, and plenty of well-decayed manure and leaf-mould forked in. This is a once-only chance of really feeding plants that it is hoped will remain in position for years. They should be planted about 10-15 ins. apart, according to their species.

If a thick hedge is wanted, a double-staggered row can be planted about 10-12 ins. apart. The newly planted must be watered generously and not allowed to go dry through their first growing season. A 2-in. mulch of well-rotted manure in the April after planting will help to keep roots moist.

A severe winter frost often lifts the unanchored plant out of the ground, and inspection and firming up of the recently planted should be carried out from time to time.

Pruning

Clipping a hedge is by no means easy and few of us have the straight eye required to carry out the work in a satisfactory way without a string line or some form of guidance.

The art is to cut upwards, pyramidally so that the top of the hedge does not overhang and overshadow the bottom. If it does, the base of the hedge will suffer and die away.

Flowering hedges should be trimmed back as the flowers fade, but the majority of hedges are best cut back in May and August; then, growing little through the winter, they remain neat and tidy until the spring.

If you can only manage one cut a year, then do the work in August or September. The neglected hedge that requires drastic clipping, possibly cutting back to within 6 ins. of the ground, should be dealt with in April.

The gardener should take the opportunity after clipping of thoroughly cleaning up and weeding the base of the hedge, for it is here that pests congregate and disease spreads. A spray with an insecticide may be a wise precaution.

Warnings

Gardeners anxious to shut out their neighbour at lightning speed should beware. Their request for a thick and impenetrable hedge (and if prickly so much the better) reaching to some 6 ft. is not to be fulfilled at a moment's notice.

It is a mistake to flog the young hedge with fertilizers, for if it grows more than a foot a year it may well get thin and spindly, fading away at the base.

My second warning is to those with a very small garden. Hedges take up a great deal of room and deprive other plants of food, sun, light and air. The Privet is not the only greedy subject and few plants prosper alongside a hedge.

Young hedges need constant training and attention; veterans have usually learned the way they should grow.

Cutting back is an important chore, for the well-trimmed will stand up to wind and snow and live long.

14 Climbers

Nature intended climbers to cover trees, not awkwardly shaped houses, walls, pergolas and eyesores, and few of them are equipped to do so other than the Ivy, Virginian Creeper, *Hydrangea petiolaris* and *Schizophragma integrifolium*.

There is a far larger number of non-self-supporting subjects, without tendrils, spines or aerial shoots, that will twine and festoon as required if given assistance, besides a diversity of wall plants to choose from.

Aspect is of premier importance when deciding upon which climber to grow, and the south and south-west walls, being favoured with the maximum hours of sunshine, should be reserved for the gardener's favourites, remembering that they are the only walls where the tender such as Abutilon, Actinidia and Passion Flower are likely to survive. The north wall is often a problem, few subjects being able to manage with such limited sunshine.

Plants grown on pergolas need to be specially hardy, but provided the pergola is well-built with supporting pillars (of old brick whenever possible), then roses will cover the construction and act as host to the clematis.

Planting

Climbers are naturally hungry plants and the soil must be well prepared, deeply dug and generously enriched with manure if the plant is to travel fast and far.

The climber will need support. If the walls are wired, then galvanized wall-eyes must be used to keep the wire away from the face of the wall for at least four or five inches.

Wall nails with soft leaden strip heads that can be bent around the plant's stem are easy to use but loosen the pointing.

Gardeners without wall, fence or tree-stump will find that the Yew, Holly, Pyracantha, Laburnum or old fruit tree will act as hospitable hosts to the climber without harm to themselves. The clematis looks especially beautiful when twining through a neighbour.

If a climber is asked to mount a stake, pole or bole of a tree, then it can be given help in the early stages of its ascent by covering the support with wire-netting.

When it comes to planting, keep the climber at least a foot away from the wall so that the stem turns in at an angle. If placed too close to the wall, the climber will miss the benefit of the rain and will have to be copiously watered. The wall, being porous, will compete for the moisture.

A newly-planted climber should not be disciplined by strict ties until the soil has settled. It must, however, be loosely held to the support temporarily so that the stem is not swayed or damaged by the wind.

Here follows a list of climbing plants, giving their special preferences for aspect.

Actinidia (Chinese Gooseberry) is a star turn. *A. chinensis* has heart-shaped leaves with shoots covered with innumerable red hairs. The creamy flowers come in clusters and are followed by fruit which, I am told, is edible. (S. and S.W.)

A. kolomikta is even more remarkable and its tricoloured variegated leaves are a wonder, the terminal half being suffused white and pink. However, the performance is only half-hearted unless given full sun.

Akebia has chocolate-purple May flowers that are followed by interesting sausage-shaped fruits grey-violet in colour: it is twining and vigorous. (S.W.)

Ampelopsis, a member of the Vitis or Vine family, was until lately the catalogue name for the Virginian Creeper. These two are now botanically separated and the true Virginian Creeper will now be found under its new name, *Parthenocissus quinquefolia.*

I understand that one of the reasons for the divorce was that the Ampelopsis genus of deciduous climbers (and there are six or more of them) differ from the Virginia Creeper in having free petals and usually compound leaves.

A. brevipedunculata has foliage not unlike the Hop and, after a good summer, bears delightful small porcelain-blue grapes.

These plants are best bought in pots; they are self-clinging and easy-going on most walls.

Aristolochia (Dutchman's Pipe) has brown-yellow pipe-shaped flowers and heart-shaped leaves.

A. durior is a rampant grower and its flowers are apt to be hidden by abundant foliage. (N.W. and E.)

Asteranthera ovata is a self-supporting creeper that is quite happy trailing on the ground providing it is a very mild district. Its red tubular flowers are attractive, the lower lip being red-veined and the throat white. (S. and S.W.)

Berberidopsis corallina (Coral Plant), with heart-shaped leaves and pendant racemes of coral-crimson flowers, needs shelter, partial shade and has a strong dislike of chalk. It appreciates the support of a neighbour creeper on a west wall. It is a beauty if it likes you.

Bignonia, also known as Campsis or Tecoma, is the Trumpet Vine. *B. radicans* is self-clinging and presents orange trumpet flowers in late summer. Catalogued as hardy in southern counties only, I have seen this climber flowering profusely in Colchester, Suffolk. There are no cast-iron rules for plants. (S. and S.W.)

Now we come to the important **Clematis** family.

The south wall may prove too hot for them unless their roots are protected from the sun. The majority will enjoy the south-west or sheltered west wall. A few, mainly members of the strong *C. montana* group, have the vigour to stand up to the conditions of a north wall.

An ordinary good and well-drained soil with a taste of mortar rubble and a forkful of rotted manure at the bottom of the planting hole will suit the Clematis.

Plants are usually sold in pots and can be planted at any time, but are best transplanted in the early autumn or spring.

Pruning depends upon variety, and here the gardener will find the Clematis specialist's catalogue helpful in giving precise information as to the best pruning dates for the different sections, to one of which each variety belongs.

Meanwhile, as a rough guide, Mr Fisk of Westleton Nurseries suggests the amateur should prune hard in February those that bloom late in the season, that is from July onwards, leaving those that bloom before July, alone. But plants must not be allowed to become an ugly tangle and hard pruning, cutting back young shoots to within 6 ins. of older wood, is sometimes necessary.

When it comes to choosing varieties, violet-purple 'Jackmanii' and pale-mauve-pink 'Nelly Moser' seen everywhere are perhaps a trifle over-exposed, while the species other than *C. montana*, which are more distinguished and interesting and easier to grow are still unknown.

I should like to introduce to those who have not yet met them, pale purple-pink *C. chrysocoma*, not unlike *C. montana* but more delicate, and *C. tangutica*, the best yellow clematis, which gives an abundance of small lantern-shaped flowers followed by delightful feathery seed-heads.

As a change from the familiar large-flowered hybrids, I would suggest soft rose-pink 'Comtesse de Bouchard', violet 'Gipsy Queen', or the finest white of them all, 'Madame le Coultre'.

On to the **Ivy,** and no creeper clings so tight to its support as the Hedera, climbing without assistance to great heights, thriving on the meanest of soils, and putting up with shady, unpromising situations. Out of fashion at the moment, it has many qualities and a variety of forms.

H. canariensis variegata, the Canary Island Ivy, has large dark-green ovate leaves, merging into silvery-grey and bordered white: *H. chrysocarpa*, sometimes known as Emerald Green, the Italian Ivy has bright copper-coloured leaves with green veinings, and *H. colchica*, the Persian Ivy, is a lustrous dark green.

H. helix 'Buttercup' is the best golden ivy. 'Silver Queen' is outstanding too, with broadly-edged creamy-white leaves that are tinged with pink in the late autumn.

H. helix tricolor or *elegantissima* is equally attractive, with small grey-green leaves bordered white, edged in winter with rosy-pink.

If a fast grower is needed to clothe an ugly building or bare ground, then none will do it faster than *H. hibernia*, the Irish member of the family.

The Ivy has the reputation of being destructive to walls and pointing but the damage is often exaggerated. However, it should be watched. (N., E., and W.)

Gardeners who like the smell of beer will want to grow *Humulus japonicus*, the common **Hop,** and *H. j. variegatus* is certainly an attractive twining climber. The male blooms are borne in axillary panicles and female blooms in cones in clusters on separate plants; on this occasion, the female form is the most ornamental. (S., S.W. and E.) Hops should be gathered in September for drying and the plant cut down in October.

Hydrangea petiolaris is a Japanese self-clinging climber of great merit. It is suitable for any aspect, even the shady or north wall, and is a summer flowerer of character. The large, flat corymbs are surrounded by white sterile flowers.

The common white **Jasmine,** *J. officinale,* and the yellow Winter Jasmine are extremely well known and need no recommendation. But this is a large family, and *J. beesianum,* with deeprose fragrant flowers, and pale pink *J.* × *stephanense* deserve to be given more opportunities, while those living in the warm south with a sheltered wall should plant *J. polyanthum,* for the white flowers, pink inside, are the sweetest-scented of them all.

The Jasmine flowers best in full sun. (S. and S.W.)

Lonicera, the Climbing Honeysuckle, enjoys good ordinary fare and plenty of sun, but, like the Clematis, its roots prefer to be in the shade. These are rambling rather than climbing subjects and do better in freedom disguising an unwanted tree or ugly building than restricted to a wall.

Again, there are a number of Honeysuckles that are too seldom seen and unfortunately too many indifferent varieties offered at some of the garden centres.

Some gardeners will buy for beauty and others for fragrance, for it is not always possible to get both from one plant.

However, I name a few that do fill the double bill.

Lonicera × *americana* is vigorous and free-flowering and its white flowers that pass to yellow and then become tinged with purple give a spectacular display. *L. japonica halliana* has white flowers changing to yellow, and *L. japonica repens* (*L. flexuosa*) yellow flowers stained purple.

L. periclymenum, the yellow Woodbine of the hedgerow, needs no description. *L. p. belgica* has flowers flushed red-purple, while

L. p. serotina, the Dutch Honeysuckle, is orange-red. All these have both good looks and heavenly scent.

Gardeners only concerned with appearance will be pleased with *L. × brownii*, the scarlet trumpet honeysuckle with orange-scarlet flowers, or *L. tragophylla*, canary-yellow-flowering, that comes from China, and being sun-shy requires shade.

L. fragrantissima, the partially evergreen Chinese honeysuckle, excites interest, flowering as it does from December to March. Growing to some 6 ft., its winter cream-coloured flowers are sweetly fragrant. Tied in with discretion in the autumn, *L. fragrantissima* will make a delightful bush or wall plant on a south-east wall in the milder counties. (S., W. and E.)

Passiflora or Passion Flower is a half-hardy for a south or south-west wall; the base of the plant should be given protection with straw or bracken during severe weather.

The Passion Flower will be found willing, given a sheltered position and good ordinary soil with a taste of well-rotted manure. It is best pruned by shortening small shoots to 5 or 6 ins. in February and the strong ones to 2 or 3 ft. Only a limited amount of old wood should be allowed.

P. caerulea is the blue Passion Flower, and 'Constance Elliott' is its lovely white form. The showy red varieties should be left to the conservatory.

As I am constantly asked for the interpretation of the exotic structure of the Passiflora flower, I give it here.

The ten petals and sepals represent the ten disciples, leaving out Judas and Doubting Thomas. The corona represents the Crown of Thorns, the five stamens the Wounds and the three stigmas the nails. The hand-like leaves represent the hand of the tormentors of Jesus, and the tendrils the whip with which He was scourged.

There is nothing much to be said about the **Periploca**, the Silk Vine, other than that *P. graeca* is a twisting climber of pleasant texture which will grow with ease to 40 ft., the leaves often hiding the rather uninteresting purple-brown summer flowers.

Polygonum baldschuanicum, the Russian Vine and mile-a-minute climber, is too often looked upon with disdain. Left to its rampant self, it is a menace, but cared for and severely cut back in spring, its feathery white panicles can be most effective. It does a grand job in covering the unsightly and many a hideous shack is the better for its presence.

Pyracantha, Pyrus and **Roses** are dealt with elsewhere.

Solanum, with potato-like summer flowers, is slightly tender, seems to prefer a trellis to a wall, and must be given a south or south-west aspect.

S. crispum has abundant clusters of blue flowers with pronounced orange stamens and has suddenly come into fashion in mild areas.

S. jasminoides album has sprays of white flowers and is equally attractive.

The **Vitis** genus, which includes the ornamental vines, are desirable for their wonderful autumnal foliage. The self-clinging should be reserved for walls and the tendril-climbing kept for balustrades, pergolas and so on.

This is a family with a wealth of variation described in nursery-men's catalogues and in particular in that of Hillier's of Winchester.

However, I must mention *V. coignetiae*, a Japanese species and to my mind the best of them all, with its gorgeous orange and crimson leaves at the turn of the year.

If ornamental fruit is wanted, then the gardener should turn to *V. vinifera*, the Grape Vine, and its varieties. They do extraordinarily well in towns, with their heads in the sun and their roots in the shade of an area.

Fortunate is the gardener with an old pink wall or house festooned with **Wistaria sinensis** with drooping racemes of blue or *S. alba*, white. How lucky we are that this splendid climber grows so well in town.

W. floribunda rosea is a rose-pink that will please, while *W. venusta*, a large white Japanese species, has special charm and a delicate fragrance. Here is yet another sun-lover, happy in a rich sandy loam; it should be pruned in January or February, shortening shoots not required for extending branches to within an inch of their base. (S. and S.W.)

15 Perennials

The herbaceous border, a very beautiful Edwardian institution, is fast disappearing. In many gardens where borders were kept strictly to herbaceous subjects there was neither the money nor the men to keep them going, and they were replaced by the mixed border.

We have not lost much by the change-over, for by admitting the entry of bulbs and shrubs we have prolonged the flowering season, and the roses, annuals and bedding plants add colour while we are now spared the tiresome lifting, dividing and replanting every three years that the herbaceous border demanded, besides the endless summer staking.

In this chapter, I deal with the perennials that will be needed for the herbaceous or mixed border. And here the study of the leading nurserymen's catalogues will be found extremely helpful.

The perennial is a plant that has a life-span of over two years. It loses its foliage in the autumn and dies down but its rootstock remains alive throwing up fresh growth in the spring.

Width, Gradation and Spacing

When deciding the width of the border it should be remembered that the very narrow bed of less than six feet is seldom successful unless it has an interesting background. The planter should beware of the skimpy look that can result from lack of depth.

The herbaceous border of the past was strictly planted according to height, with the Delphiniums and Hollyhocks at the back and each subject regimented according to its height in steps.

We have lost the taste for this uniform planting and have learnt the value of the broken and undulating line; the brash will deliberately introduce a giant six-footer in the front row alongside a creeper or London Pride.

This does not always come off but it is a pleasant change from the traditional and rather boring gentle gradation.

When it comes to spacing, the gardener who does not know the habit of the plant may find even a rough guide helpful: I suggest small plants should be kept 7-8 ins. apart, medium plants 15 ins. apart and the tall subjects about 2 ft. apart, the aim being to hide the earth without overcrowding.

The value of planting groups of a particular plant rather than planting one or two together is now generally accepted. One needs from three or four to a dozen or so of a plant according to the size of the border to make a real effect. It is important that more space should be allowed between these groups or drifts than between individual plants.

The Mini-border

It is noticeable that a greater proportion of dwarf subjects is being grown in order to avoid staking and mini-borders are already fashionable. Mr Alan Bloom of Bressingham Nurseries has introduced gardeners to a number of dwarf varieties of distinguished hardy plants suitable for the mini-border. The list that follows is his selection:

Achillea 'Moonshine': the bright yellow heads do not fade. 2 ft.

Anaphalis triplinervis: a slow-growing dwarf. 2 ft.

Armeria 'Bloodstone': rosy crimson. 12 ins.

Aster dwarf 'Novae Belgii' variety: double violet-purple. 12 ins.

Campanula glomerata dahurica 'Purple Pixie': a late summer violet-purple flowerer of perfect form. 15 ins.

C. lactiflora: in shades of light blue. 3 ft.

C. persicifolia: grown from selected seed. 2 ft.

C. trachelium bernice: double powder-blue flowers. 2 ft.

Centaurea hypoleuca: pale pink, dwarf habit. 18 ins.

Coreopsis verticillata grandiflora: large starry-yellow flowers. 2 ft.

Dianthus 'Isolde': a speckled maroon and pink Border Pink. 18 ins.

Doronicum 'Spring Beauty' ('Frühlingspracht'): fully double deep-yellow flowers. 18 ins.

Erigeron 'Prosperity': almost double, mauve-blue flowers. 18 ins.

Euphorbia epithymoides (syn. *polychroma*): lemon flowers in early spring. 18 ins.

Geum × *borisii*: neat habit, bright orange flowers. 12 ins.

Heuchera Bressingham Hybrids: excellent strain in shades from palest pink to deep crimson. 2 ft.

Inula 'Golden Beauty': bushes of yellow flowers, long-flowering season. 2 ft.

Liatris 'Kobold' (syn. *spicata montana*): intense lilac. 2 ft.

Phlox 'Gnome': pink flowers, dwarf habit. 2 ft.

Polygonum 'Lowndes Variety': useful ground cover plant. 10 ins.

Potentilla 'Gibson's Scarlet': vivid single red flowers. 12 ins.

Rudbeckia 'Goldsturm': deep-yellow, black-centred flowers. 2 ft.

Salvia 'East Friesland': dwarf form. 18 ins.

Sedum spectabile 'Autumn Joy' ('Herbstfreude'): massive heads of bright rose-salmon flowers tinged bronze. 1½-2 ft.

Veronica 'Saraband': vigorous grey foliage, erect spikes of deep violet-blue. 20 ins.

Colour and Texture

It is said that flowers cannot clash and that Nature can do no wrong. This is far from true, and I have caught vermilion 'Super Star', wonderful rose that it is, madly clashing with orange Alstroemerias and half a dozen others in one afternoon.

Successful planting is a question of finding happy flower partnerships, such as Pinks with silver foliage, blue Grape Hyacinths carpeting *Magnolia stellata*, or scarlet *Lobelia fulgens* alongside a cloud of white Gypsophila with grey Lamb's Ear and white Violas in the offing. On the whole, when planning colour harmonies, I prefer convivial trios or even foursomes to pairs.

Some gardeners will plan for a succession of colour throughout the year; others, who are to be away either for the winter or summer, will give the plants likely to flower in their absence a miss.

Fuchsias galore in a town garden

A 'Garden of Illusion', showing an imaginative use of mirrors

There are gardeners who will plant a blue, red and orange or the ever-popular white garden; a number will concentrate on growing a particular genus, Roses, Lilies, Iris or Ferns, while the flower-arranger will search not only for the beautiful, but for the striking, comic or odd.

Colour is a delight but there will be some who will put fragrance first, and here, alas, among herbaceous subjects, the choice is not as extensive as one might wish. Phlox has to my mind a superb scent, but here not everyone will agree with me, which is no doubt the reason why it has not been used commercially.

The gardener should have no difficulty in keeping his border colourful from March to November, with high peaks from June to September. Frugal patches are inevitable and perhaps a blessing, for there is such a thing as too much colour and a flowerless lull after the blaze of annuals and bedding plants can be a welcome return to restful greenery.

Gertrude Jekyll gave us invaluable tips on planting, noting that whereas all the strong warm colours—deep yellow, orange, scarlet, crimson and any deeper kinds of rich colourings—are best suited for a gradual progression of intermingling shades, the cool colours and pure blue especially demand a contrast.

A good supply of colour variations is available even to the town gardener and there is no real excuse for allowing scarlet 'Paul Crampel' geraniums and Oxford-blue Lobelia to dominate the scene.

Buying

The flower-shows give the gardener an opportunity of getting acquainted not only with the plants but with the nurseryman. The professional horticulturist is almost invariably anxious to be helpful.

The importance of buying good cannot be over-emphazised. The bargain-hunter often finds himself in charge of a rag-bag collection of inferior plants.

We cannot all have the imaginative taste of a Vita Sackville-West, the inspirator of Sissinghurst, but we can follow her invariable practice of not only growing the best plants, but choosing also the best varieties.

The novice must not allow himself to be carried away by the flashy performance of a newcomer but should go for the plants that are known for their garden-worthiness. A plant can only show reliability after a certain number of years of cultivation. A few new introductions are fun, but the well-tried should be the mainstay of a new garden.

Textures can be as exciting as colour, and the spiky Agave, Yucca, or New Zealand Flax with its erect sword-like leaves are particularly telling.

Shrubs, among them the Irish Yew, shrub roses such as the lovely 'Nevada' or 'China Town', and outstanding bulbs such as the white Daffodils and Lily Tulips can play an important part in a mixed planting, but there is no scarcity of choice. Permanent plantings of shrubs clearly save time and labour.

Border Care

After-care of a well-prepared border consists of regular hoeing to keep a fine tilth and to dismiss the weeds, skilful and—so far as is possible—invisible and early staking of those that have not the stamina to stand on their own, and making sure that no plant dies through lack of water.

Watering is a problem, and there is truth in the veteran's saying that once you start you must go on. However, there is the alternative, mulching.

This is an excellent way of conserving moisture if carried out after a downpour of rain, and also acts as a feed. If it creates a heaven for the slugs and others, then war must be declared against them with bran and methaldehyde.

Regular deadheading is essential, otherwise the plants' energy will be spent on reproduction. Some plants will give their all and then depart.

Growth thinning is in most cases unnecessary, but Delphiniums and Michaelmas Daisies give a far better display if the number of their stems is limited to three or four.

When late autumn arrives, the decision has to be made whether to cut down the brown stems and tidy up or leave things as they are until the spring for winter protection.

The decision is a simple one. If the garden is in a cold and exposed position, the protection will be valuable, in warm parts of the country there is no excuse for the border being anything but spick and span.

Winter care is light. Plants lifted by the frost, particularly the newly planted, should be trodden back into place, a few bracken fronds or straw scattered around the delicate, and perhaps a rampant grower taught to keep its place.

I now give a list of the best perennials for towns (by no means London only).

Acanthus (Bear's Breeches) is a handsome plant used by the Greeks and Romans in their classical and Corinthian decorations. The leaves are thistle-like and the tubular flower a dull pink-red purple.

A. longifolius is freer flowering than the popular *A. mollis*. June-Aug. 3 ft.

Achillea (Yarrow). Here *A. filipendulina* is a fine group and 'Gold Plate', with its flat, flashy yellow heads on stiff stems, is particularly good for cutting and drying. July-Aug. 4-5 ft. But some will prefer the quieter pale yellow *A. taygetea*. 18 ins.

A. ptarmica (Pearl), a double white button-like flower that comes in clusters, is accommodating. June-Aug. 3 ft.

Aconitum (Monkshood) bears erect spikes of blue or purple-blue hooded flowers. A plant that resents disturbance and may take a little time to settle down. June-Aug. 3-5 ft.

'Blue Sceptre' *variegata bicolor*, has blue and white flowers. July-Aug. 2 ft.

Ajuga (Bugle), one of the best ground-covering plants we have, not being averse to shade and doing well on heavy soil. *A. pyramidalis* has gentian blue flowers and is the best for colour. April-June. 9 ins.

A. reptans alba has white flowers, while *A. r. multicolour*, known as Rainbow, is a marbled foliage plant of dark red-purple and yellow. June-July. 6-12 ins.

Alchemilla is another carpeting plant and labour-saver. The wild plant with appealing soft green foliage and sulphur-green flowers is known as Lady's Mantle. *A. mollis* has green straw-yellow flowers in bloom most of the summer. 12 ins.

Alstroemeria. This is the Peruvian Lily with orange flowers speckled black, a free and easy subject. July-Aug. 3 ft.

But when it comes to the *A. ligtu* hybrids, it is a different tale, for they can be remarkably difficult. In any case, they must be given perfect conditions—ideal drainage, rich soil, warm aspect and their ropy roots require careful planting by green fingers. Nurserymen often note in their catalogue that 'owing to the hazards which exist beyond their control, they cannot undertake replacements should losses occur.' These words speak for themselves.

However, having given this serious warning, let me add that the large flower-heads of pink, salmon, apricot and flame are beautiful and worth a struggle. The risk is reduced if the gardener invests in eighteen-months-old pot-grown plants and has them delivered in the spring. A little protection during the first winter is a wise safety precaution.

If the Ligtus like you they will spread underground and break out here and there with increasing energy as the years go by.

Some gardeners prefer to raise these temperamentals from seed.

Alyssum (Madwort—said to cure hydrophobia—or Gold Dust). The perennial variety *A. saxatile* is a showy sun-lover to be had in biscuit, light yellow and gold. Rather too large for the true rockery, this plant is best seen in the border and, for a pleasant change, out of the company of Aubrietia and Arabis.

Anaphalis, the everlasting flower with grey foliage. *A. triplinervis* is a slow-growing dwarf with hairy woolly leaves and white immortelles in August. 12 ins.

Anchusa, a useful blue early flowerer that looks well among the pyrethrums. *A. azurea* is usually the nost rewarding group so long as young plants are raised annually ready to take the place of the middle-aged. 'Little John' is a dwarf of 2 ft., 'Opal' is the best light blue, while 'Royal Blue' is large and an intense gentian shade. Summer. 3-5 ft.

Anemone. This is the wind-flower family, too varied for generalization. The best-known herbaceous species is *A. hupehensis iaponica*, with vine-like leaves and saucer-shaped pink and white flowers. A slow starter but a splendid town plant once settled in. Deep pink 'Queen Charlotte' is well liked; 'Louise Uhink' is the pick of the whites. Sept.-Oct. 3½ ft.

Little *A. pulsatilla* (Pasque Flower), with lovely silky violet-mauve flowers and fern-like foliage, now referred to as *Pulsatilla*

vulgaris, adds charm to the spring border. April-May. 12 ins.
Antennaria (Cat's-Ear), a carpet, wall or crevice plant, has silvery foliage and pink flowers. Summer. 3-4 ins.

Anthemis, an easy doer with yellow or white daisy-like flowers. Plants are best cut down immediately after flowering so that they have time to make protective young growth before the winter. Golden-yellow 'Grallagh Gold' leads the list. July-Aug. 3 ft.

Aquilegia (Columbine) enjoys the sun but lasts longer in bloom if planted in partial shade. It is a little fussy about both drought and sogginess. The long-spurred and other garden forms are to be had in many different colours. 'Crimson Star', bright crimson and white, and 'Sky Blue' are two favourites. May. 2½ ft.

Arabis, an easily grown single, but sometimes a temperamental double in towns, is a large white rockery plant with grey-green foliage that needs to be kept under control. *A. albida coccinea* with crimson flowers should be more seen. May. 6 ins.

Armeria (Thrift), a sun-lover with round heads and grass-like foliage, making delightful small tussocks. *A. maritima* is the sea pink, 6 ins. *A. m. alba* is the albina form, and 'Vindictive' a crimson red. May-June. 9 ins.

Asperula is another small hummock plant—pink flowers—neat green hummocks worthy of a place in the very front of the border when there is no rockery.

Aster. *A. amellus*, the bushy sturdy Michaelmas Daisy that is best planted in the spring. 'King George' is a fine deep blue and 'Sonia' the best pink. This group is slower growing than the majority of Michaelmas Daisies. Aug.-Oct. 2-2½ ft.

A. novi belgii is the New York aster. One-year-old plants give a superior performance to divisions from clumps. This group has for years played an important part in the autumn border. Rosy-red 'Alpenglow', 'Little Boy Blue', violet 'Royal Velvet' and rosy-pink 'Winsome Winnie' are among the best. Sept. 2½ ft.

A. yunnanensis napsbury, with large single flowers to a stem of a brilliant deep blue, is perhaps the star of the family. June. 18 ins.

Astilbe (Goatsbeard), often confused with Spiraea, has feathery plumes in bright pinks, reds and crimsons, pale shades and white. It needs a cool moist place and benefits by being planted in peat, or mulched with well-rotted dung to conserve the moisture. Rose-pink 'Granat' is a graceful plant. June-July. 3 ft.

Aubrietia (the coloured Rock Cress), mauve, purple, pink or crimson, and an excellent rockery or wall plant. A general favourite that must be severely trimmed back after flowering and top-dressed, otherwise it becomes a straggler. Wallflower-red 'Mrs Rodewald' is outstanding. April-May.

Bellis, the little Double Daisy. China rose 'Dresden China' and red 'Rob Roy' still head the list. Spring. 3 ins.

Bergenia cordifolia (*Megasea*), a member of the saxifrage family known to many gardeners as border plant or weed smotherer, with pink flowers on stout stems and large round leaves which gave it the nick-name Elephant's Ears. March-April. 15 ins.

Campanula. This is a tremendous genus, diverse in form, of which I mention but a few. It is surprising that there is not a Campanula Society to keep us in touch and informed about this much-loved plant. Perhaps I may encourage a Campanula fan to pioneer such a Society?

C. glomerata dahurica is impressive, with globular heads of violet. June. 2 ft. *C. lactiflora* has effective light blue spikes. June-Aug. 3 ft. *C. l.* 'Loddon Anna' is a lovely flesh-pink form, 3-4 ft., while *C. l.* 'Pouffe' makes neat mounds of light blue flowers of 9 ins. *C. latifolia alba* with spikes of white bells has many admirers. 3 ft. But *C. persicifolia* holds its place as one of the best of the clan with delightful slender stems and nodding bells. Blue 'Telham Beauty' and glistening white 'Fleur de Neige' are splendid if well fed but kept in check. June-Aug. 3 ft.

Centaurea (Perennial Cornflower) is useful because of its long flowering period and silvery-grey foliage. *C. dealbata* 'John Coutts' is a new bright pink introduction. 2 ft. Cornflower lovers should get to know some of the perennials, of which there are a number, among them pink *rigidifolia*. June-Sept. 2 ft.

Centranthus ruber atro coccineus (Red Valerian) that grows so bravely on a dry wall. A plant that will survive in the most unpromising positions so long as there is good drainage. A white form is also available. July. 2-3 ft.

Cephalaria (Giant Scabious). *C. tartarica* is pale yellow and, being tall, requires space to look effective. June-July. 5-6 ft.

Chrysanthemum maximum (Ox-Eye or Shasta Daisy), white single or double. There are hybrids such as white double

'Esther Read', white anemone-centred 'Wirral Pride', and 'Wirral Supreme', the strongest grower of the group. The hybrids are apt to die out during a difficult winter. Offsets and cuttings should be taken in the summer ready to fill the gaps.

The Korean, Cushion and Rubellum Chrysanthemums are of great service to the town gardener, if the more hardy varieties are chosen. Koreans 'Gold Dust' and 'Tapestry Rose' usually do well and if hard frosts damage open flowers, unopened buds often come out unharmed. Beautiful 'Wedding Day', glistening white with green centres, unfortunately flowers late and really needs glass protection to be seen at its best. Sept.-Oct. 2½-3 ft.

The **Pyrethrum** belongs to the chrysanthemum family and demands a well-drained, light soil, otherwise casualties must be expected, especially among the doubles. After the first crop of bloom, the plant should be cut down to encourage a second performance. 'Avalanche' is the best white single, and bright cerise 'Brenda' a fine plant. May-June. 2½ ft.

Convallaria (Lily of the Valley), well-loved but often neglected for it needs good fare to be at its best. Rich moist soil is what is wanted, without disturbance. 'Fortin's Giant' is still the finest variety. The rather scarce pink Lily of the Valley is much over-rated. June. 8 ins.

Coreopsis, a yellow daisy flower, is inclined to be untidy in the border but is excellent for cutting. 'Mayfield Giant', *C. grandiflora* 'Perry's Variety' and 'Baden Gold' all flower freely if given sun and kept to starvation diet. 2-3 ft. But for those who are looking for a neat grower, *C. verticillata*, less known but with fern-like foliage and small star-like flowers, is a wiser choice. 18 ins.

Corydalis cheilanthifolia, the yellow Fumitory from China, has fern-like foliage, and is a useful plant for growing in fissures in old walls and barren stony places where others fail. *C. lutea* can be a menace, being invasive and seeding itself too freely. Summer. 12 ins.

Dahlia. Never has this half-hardy herbaceous tuberous-rooted perennial been more popular than it is today. It was first introduced in 1789 from Central America and Mexico, and varieties are now legion.

Tubers are best started in pots planted 2 ins. deep in March or April in a temperature of about 55°F. and then planted out in the third week of May or the beginning of June if the weather is unfavourable.

It is important to limit the number of shoots in July and to mulch the plants well in early summer to keep the roots cool and moist.

The tubers should be lifted in the autumn when the top growth is blackened by the frost, and stored in a frostproof, airy place where there is sufficient moisture in the air to prevent the tubers from shrivelling.

Among the groups of varieties recently classified there are the single anemone-flowered, collarette and paeony-flowered: the giant, large, medium, small and miniature decoratives: the ball dahlias (divided into two sections): the pompom: the cactus and semi-cactus: and the orchid-flowered.

The less known anemone-flowered and collarettes are remarkably attractive.

It must be remembered that the Dahlia is a gross feeder and drinker. Nitrogenous fertilizers, however, should be avoided, as they lead to greenery rather than flowers.

Secure staking, by driving strong supports into the ground, is vital.

Town gardeners should be encouraged by the fact that many of the successful exhibitors at the shows come from town and suburban areas. July-Sept. 2-5 ft.

Delphinium. This is the perennial larkspur named after the dolphin, the unexpanded buds having reminded some ancient botanist of the fish.

It is its colour that excels; there are splendid dark and light blues, the modern 'shot' mixtures, the whites (with or without black eyes), the blush pinks and reds, while the much-discussed raspberry introduction will either please or displease.

The newcomers have in the main tremendous stamina, with thick broomstick stems, but have mislaid some of the grace of the former varieties that swayed in the breeze. However, the modern trend is to reduce height and the 3 ft. Belladonna hybrids and dwarf varieties are ideal for backyard gardens, and good lasters.

Staking, particularly of the opulent spikes, and deadheading are important. If the plant is cut back to the ground after flowering and well mulched, it may give a second performance.

A good loam enriched with rotted manure, a sunny position,

and plenty of air and elbow room are the plant's main requirements, for the Delphinium is vulnerable to mildew.

When winter comes the crown must be protected with sharp sand against slugs.

There are specialist Delphinium growers, among them Blackmore and Langdon of Bath, and Baker's of Codsall, who have impressive collections of the large-flowered hybrids, while excellent results are to be had from a specialist's packet of seed. Plants are usually best bought in the spring. June-July. 4-6 ft.

Dianthus is a great garden family that includes the Border Carnation and Garden Pink. They can be grown successfully without pampering, provided they are given an open, sunny position, and a well-drained alkaline soil with an addition of mortar rubble.

A sprinkling of lime should be part of the spring routine and, on heavy ground, beds are best raised.

Layers and cuttings should be regularly taken from late July until the middle of August, for the Dianthus is not always long-lived.

The Border Carnation includes the flake, bizarre, picotee, fancies and selfs. I have always found the yellow and selfs rather tricky and would advise a novice to get to know the more easy-going before attempting them.

The Pink, unlike the border carnation, is usually possessed of a winning 'eye' or dark central zone.

A catalogue from a Dianthus specialist should be consulted but I would like to recommend 'Doris', a soft salmon with an azalea-red centre, white double 'Mrs Sinkins', a veteran with incomparable scent, and 'Dad's Favourite', a white-laced chocolate double, or a mat of Cheddar Pinks for the top of a friendly wall.

The Border Carnation puts all its energy into one June or early July flowering. 1 ft. The Pink flowers in June, but the flowering period can be prolonged by constant deadheading. 10 ins.

Dicentra (Bleeding Heart, Lyre Flower or Dutchman's Breeches), has arching stems festooned with pink and white locket-shaped flowers.

An easy and lovely plant, enjoying a light, rich soil, that will grow in a semi-shaded corner where others fail to flower, provided there is good drainage.

In cold areas the Dicentra benefits by a protective covering of ashes or old manure. In drought the fine-cut foliage is apt to die back and dust-dry corners should be avoided.

This is an enduring, long-lived plant that can be propagated by cuttings taken with a heel or by division when resting.

Bountiful, with slightly glaucous foliage, flowers from April to September, and desirable because of its long flowering period, *Dicentra* 'Adrian Bloom', a newcomer, is of a slightly brighter crimson, while *D. spectabilis*, with large rosy-crimson and white flowers, is still among the most desirable varieties of the family. May. 2 ft.

Dictamus (Burning Bush), capable of secreting volatile oil that on a windless, warm day can be ignited with a lighted match. Likes a semi-shady position and a good ordinary soil.

D. alba has spikes of white and *D. purpureus* rosy-purple flowers. June-July. 2 ft.

Digitalis (Foxglove). The woodland Foxglove is a biennial but there are several perennial species, such as *D. ambigua*, dull yellow blotched brown; but even these are better treated as biennials in towns. July-Aug. 2 ft.

Doronicum (Leopard's Bane), one of the earliest and gayest perennials to flower, with bright green heart-shaped leaves. A sun-lover that looks well naturalized in the grass or informal garden.

D. 'Harpur Crewe', (syn. 'Excelsium') 3 ft., and 'Miss Mason', 2 ft., are both delightful, with bright yellow daisy-like flowers. Deep yellow 'Spring Beauty', fully double, is a more recent German variety. Late April and May. 18 ins.

Epimedium (Bishop's Hat) has green leaves margined with coppery bronze that are retained throughout the winter. It appreciates woodland conditions, providing good ground cover in shaded places. Plants should be divided from time to time after flowering, otherwise they become dense and matted.

E. pinnatum colchicum has yellow and *E.* × *rubrum* red flowers. June-July. 8-12 ins.

Erigeron (Fleabane), requiring light, well-drained soil and plenty of sun: averse to cold and exposed gardens.

Among garden varieties worth noting are violet-blue 'Dignity', cerise-pink 'Foerster's Liebling', an upright grower, and light-blue-mauve 'Sincerity'. July-Aug. 2-2½ ft.

Ferns, adaptable and hardy, are an asset to a town garden. Although they revel in the moist, cool woodland, if treated to peat and leaf-mould and the shade of a north wall they will soon establish themselves, provided the atmosphere is not too dry. The green fronds make a feathery frame to bright annuals and biennials.

A clay soil should be lightened by digging in sharp sand and grit; a light soil enriched by digging in good compost and well-rotted leaf-mould or peat. Dung should be avoided.

If growing ferns under trees, interfering surface roots should be cut back so that they do not cause disturbance to the fernery. A light dressing of bone-meal or general organic fertilizer should be given in the spring and old fronds trimmed back when young ones appear.

Among the ferns there are lime-lovers, lime-haters, and indifferent members of the family that will grow in both acid and alkaline soils. The fern specialist should be consulted for there are deciduous, evergreen, epyphitic and aquatic types from which to choose.

Nearly all of them prefer dappled shade but a few with thick leaves tolerate a limited amount of sun; unfortunately the more glamorous demand humidity.

However, I have known *Phyllitis scolopendrium*, the common Hartstongue with undivided ribbon-shaped leaves, a lime-lover that appreciates a taste of clay, survive and cheer a London basement in the company of Creeping Jenny.

The best planting months are April and October. The fern has no flower and is therefore seedless, plants reproducing themselves by means of spores. These are of a darkish brown and are to be found in group formation on the underside of the leaves.

Funkia, *see* Hosta.

Gaillardia (Blanket Flower). The perennials are derived from *G. aristata*. They have daisy-like flowers in different shades of red and yellow. These sunlovers do well on poor soil. 'Tommy', a tangerine self and a recent introduction, and 'Wirral Flame' are both outstanding. Summer. 2 ft.

Galega (Goat's Rue), an erect branching plant with small sweet-pea-like flowers. Lilac-blue 'Her Majesty' is one of the best of the family and will grow in unpromising places. The plant's flowering period can be increased by mulching. June-early Aug. 4 ft.

Geranium (Cranesbill). This is the true perennial geranium, not to be confused with the Pelargoniums 'Crampel' and 'Gustav Emich'.

Here is a family that deserves the enthusiastic attention of the town gardener, for the Geranium is a charming plant willing to grow and flower generously in ordinary soil if given a fairly open position. *G. endressii* 'A. T. Johnson', silver-pink, 18 ins.; 'Wargrave Pink', clear pink, 15 ins.; *G. grandiflorum*, rich blue and profuse, 15 ins.; *G. ibericum*, a neat-growing violet-blue, 2 ft; and 'Johnson's Blue', 18 ins., are all worth trying, while *G. pratense*, double-blue, 2-3 ft., is delightful.

G. sanguineum, an intense magenta-pink creeper, deserves a place in the front of the border. 9 ins. All these flower from June-Sept.

Some gardeners complain that the Geranium is invasive, but the townsman will from time to time be grateful for the plant that has the vigour to encroach.

Geum, an easy grower, single and double; fiery red 'Mrs Bradshaw' and golden-yellow 'Lady Stratheden' are leaders of the family. May. $1\frac{1}{2}$-2 ft.

Gypsophila, a lime-lover that forms a round gossamer bush of slender stems and leaves, is clouded with tiny flowers in summer. Very effective subject if planted in groups. Propagation is not easy but strong basal growths with a heel should be taken in late June, inserted in a sandy compost and kept moist under cloche. 'Bristol Fairy' is still the leading white. 'Flamingo', 'Pink Star' and semi-prostrate 'Rosy Veil' are among the best pinks. July-Sept. $1\frac{1}{2}$-3 ft.

Helenium (Sneezewort), with daisy-like flowers in yellow and shades of deep orange-red; a profuse and invaluable flowerer if given a sunny position and good soil. Summer. 2-3 ft.

Helianthemum (Sun Rose), closely allied to Rock Rose only smaller, is a happy and natural rock plant on wiry stems in a large range of colours in both single and double forms. The flowers fade fast, but others quickly take their place. The Sun Rose thrives in full sun on poor, well-drained soil. There is a long list of delightful hybrids. May-June. 12 ins.

Helianthus, the rich, yellow Sunflower. The spreading underground roots can be invasive. A plant for the back of the border that should be divided every three years. Late summer. 5-6 ft.

Helichrysum is the everlasting flower. *H. bellidioides*, with silver-white globular flowers and attractive creeping growth, should be given a warm, sunny and well-drained border.

Helleborus (Christmas Rose), a wonderful long-lasting early flowerer that should be left undisturbed. It likes a shady, well-drained position, a rich loam, and a mulch with well-decayed manure in April, and will benefit if given liquid manure occasionally during the summer.

H. argutifolius (syn. *H. corsicus*), with clusters of green flowers that last splendidly for months and glaucous green foliage, is a striking plant. 2-3 ft.

H. niger, probably the best known of the family, has pure white saucer-like flowers with golden anthers and deep green leaves but unfortunately short stalks. 12 ins.

H. orientalis is the Lenten Rose of Greece and Asia Minor, with a number of desirable varieties in creams, pinks, purples, plums, black, plain and spotted. 1½-2 ft.

Flower-arrangers favour *H. foetidus*, with pale green blooms tipped with purple, a poisonous and strong-smelling species known as Stinking Hellebore. The dark green shining foliage is deep-cut and of distinguished design. March-June. 2 ft.

Hemerocallis (Day Lily and American hobby-plant). The new hybrids range from pale yellow through orange to brilliant scarlet. They are willing growers in sun or partial shade, by the waterside or even in the water. The flowers are short-lived but there is a succession of blooms. June-Aug. 1½-3 ft.

Heracleum (Giant Cow Parsnip), dramatic with huge cartwheel flowers. At least some of the flowers should be removed if healthy foliage is wanted. Spectacular for a wild garden, this plant can be raised from March-sown seed. 7-9 ft.

Hesperis (Sweet Rocket). This is not an altogether satisfactory perennial and is most successful when allowed to naturalize itself in an informal garden. Purple or white. May-July. 2 ft.

Heuchera, a graceful fairy-like flower rather similar to London Pride with heart-shaped leaves; a plant for the front of the border. *H. sanguinea* and the Bressingham Hybrids are all charming in white, pink and shades of red.

Heucherella (Bridget Bloom—a cross between species Heuchera and *Tiarella cordifolia*) made history by winning the R.H.S. Award of Merit in 1959. Light pink, it is free-flowering. May-Oct. 18-20 ins.

Hollyhock, often treated as a biennial, is easily raised from seed sown in June, and has a gift for finding a suitable corner to sow itself. There are single, double and frilled varieties. Many colours and arresting 'Black Prince' can now be bought by separate packet. Aug.-Sept. 6-8 ft.

Hosta (syn. Funkia), the Plantain Lily, with broad leaves, green, blue-green and variegated, of immense value to the town garden. This is an excellent ground-cover foliage plant that will grow in sun or shade, and although enjoying good fare, is not particular about soil so long as it does not dry out. The tubular lilac-mauve or white flowers borne on long spikes are pleasant but by no means striking.

I give a long list of Hostas because of their splendid town tolerance.

H. var. *albo-marginata*: leaves broadly margined white. *H. crispula*: large leaves boldly veined and edged with a band of white. H. *fortunei albopicta*: tapering leaves edged pale green. *H. lancifolia*: bright green pointed leaves. *H. minor*: bright green foliage, pure white reflexed flowers. *H. sieboldiana* (syn. *glauca*): bold grey-green foliage. *H. tardiflora*: small lanceolate foliage. *H. undulata*: wavy leaves margined bright green with a centre of cream to white markings. *H. u. erromena*: robust grower with pendant flowers. *H. ventricosa*: dark green foliage, bell-shaped flowers. *H. v. aurea*: yellow-margined and particularly attractive. July-Aug. 1-3 ft.

Iberis (Perennial Candytuft). A bushy, spreading evergreen with profuse white flowers that enjoys the sun and a dry wall. May-June. 12 ins.

Iris. Here is a plant that is perfectly happy in a town garden and the modern Bearded Iris in all shades and combinations of colours are so beautiful that they deserve a planting to themselves.

They like lime, should be planted directly after flowering in a sunny position with their rhizomes almost on top of the soil so that they get baked through the summer. Clay soil should be lightened by old brick or mortar rubble.

Once in the ground, the Iris can be left for three years; it is seldom troubled by disease, given dry conditions, and is long-lived.

If overtaken by disease, infected parts should be cut away to sound flesh and replanted in a well-drained place.

A top dressing of lime in April, using 1 to 2 ozs. per square yard (builder's lime should be avoided) and a sprinkling of bonemeal, will keep the plant in good heart. Stable manure must be well-rotted or avoided. May-June. 1½-4 ft.

Iris should be planted to form clumps of the same variety for the best effect. Successful buying entails getting in touch with an Iris specialist, for many nurseries fail to supply any but the out-of-date and humdrum.

There is a flood of exciting new varieties and the new pink, brown, blue and so-termed newcomers have gained rather than lost in refinement, the falls having fewer half-markings or less striation. However, some of the stars seen at the Chelsea Show and elsewhere are shy performers and should be left to exhibitors.

The charming dwarf Bearded Iris, the Crimean and pumila groups, are perfect for the front of the border, but unfortunately they are vulnerable to wet conditions, and should not be attempted unless there is a warm, well-drained rockery or border to receive them. April-May. 4-12 ins.

As the Iris is one of the most important plants for city or town, the gardener may care to become a member of the Iris Society, which has a valuable advice bureau and organizes an annual show. The Iris is known as the poor man's orchid. I am asking that he should pay more attention to his flower.

Lastly, *I. unguicularis* (syn. *stylosa*) that flowers intermittently through the winter and is happiest planted tight against the south wall of a house. The slim pencil-shaped buds will open along with the yellow Winter Jasmine and make a delightful bouquet with the white-pink Winter Cherry.

I. unguicularis from Algeria likes a gritty, impoverished soil. Manure will merely encourage foliage. The plant resents disturbance, and, taking time to settle in, must not be allowed to dry out before becoming established. The foliage is best tied back during the summer so that the sun can get to the plant's roots. Winter. 12 ins.

I. histrioides and *reticulata*, *see* bulb chapter, p. 149.

Kniphofia (Red-hot-Poker or Torch Lily), with showy spikes on tall stems, is a plant needing sun, good soil and fast drainage. As a number of varieties are tender, winter protection should be given, tying the leaves together over the crown.

Colours range from ivory to cream-buff, orange and fiery red, and there are dwarfs and giants. Aug. 3-5 ft.

Lamium (Dead Nettle), a prostrate ground cover plant with purple flowers and nettle-shaped leaves with a central white blotch. *L. maculatum aureum*, a slow grower, has golden foliage. March. 6-10 ins.

Lavendula. Like all grey-foliage plants, lavender is town-temperamental, demanding a light and well-drained soil, winter wet often providing fatal. 'Hidcote', 15 ins., with deep blue flowers, is a useful addition the family. L. 'Munstead' is a deep blue, 1 ft., and *L. spica*, the common Old English variety with pale lavender-blue flowers, 3 ft. Young growth should be trimmed immediately after flowering. July-Aug. 1-3 ft.

Limonium (Statice or Sea Lavender) does well on sandy soil in a sunny position. *L. latifolium* has loose sprays of small lavender everlasting flowers. July-Sept. 2 ft.

Linum (Flax) requires a sheltered, warm position, only opening its flowers to the sun. It should be pruned into shape in the spring. *L. arboreum*, almost a shrub, has golden yellow flowers. *L. narbonense* is a deep blue long-laster. June-Aug. 1 ft.

Lupin. A splendid herbaceous plant content with ordinary good lime-free soil or sandy loam and a sunny or partially shaded border. It responds well to deep digging and bonemeal and a mulch of well-rotted manure in April.

The Russell Hybrids, in blue, yellow, red and orange with a number of intermediate shades besides the smokies and bicolours, are as bright as any jockey on the race-course. Tired, bedraggled, and washy blue specimens should be thrown away.

Regular deadheading is important, otherwise the plant will seed itself, and vigorous but nearly always less interesting seedlings will oust a superior but more delicate strain.

Gardeners are excused from growing this plant if they live on chalk, for the plant will never really like them.

The Tree Lupin, *L. arboreus* 'Golden Spire' and others, easily grown from a packet of seed, should not be forgotten. June-July. 3-4 ft.

Lychnis. *L. chalcedonica*, the Maltese or Jerusalem Cross, with

A roof garden in Regent's Park, London, effectively planted with bulbs

A half-acre formal garden in central London

scarlet flower-heads shaped in the form of a cross, is the brilliant member of the family. July-Aug. 3 ft. *L. coronaria*, the Rose Campion with grey foliage, has charm. June-Aug. 2½-3 ft.

L. viscaria splendens plena has bright rosy-crimson flowers and is a smaller plant, useful for the front of the border or a dry wall. All are sun-lovers, preferring a light rich loam. June-July. 12 ins.

Lysimachia (Loosestrife). *L. vulgaris* is an almost indestructible plant for a moist position. June-Aug. 2½ ft. But it is *L. nummularia aurea*, the little golden Creeping Jenny, that is the star of the loosestrife group. Summer. 4 ins.

Lythrum (Purple Loosestrife), is happy in moist places. *L. salicaria* 'Lady Sackville', bright rosy-pink, is not often seen but is a good plant. June-Sept. 2-3 ft.

Macleaya or Bocconia. *M. cordata* has white tubular flowers, while *macrocarpa* 'Coral Plume', with green-blue leaves silver below, has copper-coloured feather plumes. This is a large, impressive plant that does well in towns. Aug.-Sept. 6-8 ft.

Mimulus. Most of the musks are moisture-lovers and town gardens are often too dry for them. Their pouched flowers are red and yellow spotted and blotched. 'Whitecroft Scarlet' and 'Wisley Red' are good garden varieties. June-Sept. 4-6 ins.

Monarda (Bergamot), bushy plants with white, purple, pink and red flowers, are all easy growers given good soil and an open position. June-Sept. 2-3 ft.

Nepeta, the mauve Catmint with grey foliage, likes a well-drained soil, and gardeners on wet land should raise the bed. Young growth can be encouraged by cutting the plant back after flowering. May-Sept. 15 ins.

Oenothera (Scented Evening Primrose), with fragile flowers and red buds, needs full sun. *O. fruticosa* 'Yellow River' is splendid in the mid-border. June-Sept. 2 ft.

O. missourensis and other low-growing grey-leaved dwarfs are useful for a rockery. June-Sept. 9 ins.

Origanum vulgare aureum forms small tidy golden bushes and can be used for ground cover and foliage effect. 9 ins.

Paeonia. *P. officinalis*, the common red Peony, and its double pink and white forms do well provided they are given a sunny position and plenty of room. They like a rich soil that retains the moisture and resent disturbance. June. 3 ft.

P. Moutan (syn. *suffruticosa*) the Tree Paeony, is lovely, but more difficult and slightly tender, requiring perfect conditions. June. 4-5 ft.

Papaver (Poppy), one of the easiest plants to grow, appearing at a moment when the spring burst of bloom is fading and summer flowers not quite ready to take over. *P. orientale* is sturdy and spectacular in white, pink or scarlet blotched black within. A sun-lover that manages on the poorest of soils, it enjoys good fare but must not be allowed to encroach on less pushing neighbours. May-June. $2\frac{1}{2}$-3 ft.

P. nudicaule, the Iceland Poppy, now available in pink as well as yellow, orange and tangerine, is a much-improved plant with firm stems. July-Aug. 12-18 ins.

Penstemon. This is not an altogether hardy plant and must be given a well-drained position but not allowed to dry out in the summer. *P. heterophyllus* with blue spikes is delightful but difficult. May-June. 18 ins. *P. hartwegii* 'Garnet', deep red, would be a safer choice. July-Sept. 2 ft.

Phlox. The huge trusses of heavily-scented bloom in every colour but yellow are magnificent. The growth or 'spokes' on each plant should be limited to four or six. A partially shaded or west border suits the plant and a mulch of spent hops is advised so that roots are kept moist. Phlox should be divided every three years and the tired woody core discarded. Good soakings are important during a drought.

'White Admiral' is a splendid plant for a dark garden. Late July-Aug. $3\frac{1}{2}$ ft.

P. subulata are mat-forming rockery plants with almost stemless flowers in pink and blue-mauve. May-June. 3-5 ins.

Physostegia (Obedient Plant), so called because the flowers can be moved on the spikes and remain as placed. A useful plant that will grow in sun or partial shade. There are white and pink varieties. Aug-Sept. 2-4 ft.

Platycodon (Balloon Flower), allied to the Campanula, requires a sunny position and well-drained soil. In blue, pink and white, the buds are inflated like a balloon. July-Aug. 12-18 ins.

Polygonatum, *P. multiflorum giganteum*, Solomon's Seal or Jacob's Ladder, with arched stems and white bells, grows well in partial shade. It enjoys an annual mulch with decayed manure in March. June. 2 ft.

Polygonum (Knot Weed), has pink and red spikes in May. Pink *P. bistorta superbum* (Award of Merit 1961) is a useful showy plant. Meanwhile crimson *P. reynoutria* (18 ins.) has had plenty of publicity. May-Aug. 3 ft.

Potentilla (Cinquefoil), not unlike the Geum in yellows and scarlet, thriving in dry sunny places and poor soil. Free-flowering. June-Sept. 1-2 ft.

Primula, the native Primrose. *P. vulgaris* heads the list of a large family, and there are a number of charming coloured forms: 'Garryarde Guinevere', pink flowers and bronze leaves; 'Wanda', the popular crimson-purple, and 'Wisley Red' a telling colour with dark leaves. *P. polyanthus* now includes brilliant new strains, among them the Pacific Giants in red, pink, yellow and blue. *P. auricula*, the alpines of self-coloured velvet quality with a white or yellow eye, or the 'shows' with flowers and stems powdered white, either selfs or exotics, green, grey or white-edged. The Auricula was my hobby-plant for many years—I was an enthusiastic collector, breeder and showman, and I can thoroughly recommend 'Dusty Miller' to anyone not yet acquainted with it. May. 6-9 ins.

P. denticulata (Drumstick), with white, mauve or crimson, almost round heads, is a gay little plant. March-May. 10 ins.

Pulmonaria is a dwarf for the front of the border. *P. officinalis* has rosy flowers turning to blue, and mottled foliage, while *P. rubra* is brick-red, inclined to seed itself over-generously and smother its neighbours. March-April. 12-18 ins.

Ranunculus. *R. acris flore-pleno* has lovely double buttercup flowers, but is suitable only for warm sheltered districts. May-June. 2 ft.

Rheum. *R. rhaponticum*, the edible rhubarb with yellow leaves and red stalks, is an exciting plant and a willing grower that will brighten up a dull garden. If unwanted by the kitchen, it can be allowed to flower.

Romneya (Californian Tree Poppy) has a woody crown, blue-grey foliage and white poppy-like flowers and is a beautiful shrub-like plant. *R. coulteri* surprised me by flowering profusely in a London garden. However, disliking disturbance, it took the plant five years to settle down. A sheltered, sunny, well-drained border is essential. Aug.-Oct. 4-5 ft.

Rudbeckia (Cone Flower), is related to the sunflower. The Hirta Hybrids are a good mixed strain, ranging from crimson and bronze to deep yellow. *R. newmannii* (syn. *speciosa*), Black-Eyed Susan, is bright orange-yellow with a black centre. Aug.-Sept. 2-2½ ft.

Ruta (Rue). *R. graveolens* has yellow-green flowers and pleasant blue-grey foliage. *R.* 'Jackman's Blue' has compact and attractive blue foliage. June-Aug. 2-2½ ft.

The **Saxifraga** is a tremendous family. There are the encrusted, cushiony Kabschia or Mossy forms, all suited to the rockery. *S. umbrosa*, the much-loved London Pride, should be grown in full sun to be seen at its best. May-July. 12 ins.

Scabiosa. The *S. caucasica* varieties in different blues and white on stiff stems are excellent for cutting. This plant likes a well-drained but not too dry soil and a sunny position. It should be planted in the spring, and when established, cut back in March. Mid-blue 'Clive Greaves' is a magnificent plant but often fails in heavy soil. July-Oct. 2 ft.

Sedum (Stonecrop), a large succulent family. Varying in character, there are sunny wall-lovers, prostrate and spreading, and familiar *S. spectabile* with large flattish heads of pink and red where the butterflies are pleased to settle. A reliable plant for the front of the border. Spectacular when grown in clumps. Aug.-Sept. 18 in.

Sempervivum (Houseleek), with an array of green, rose and purple rosettes, some of them generously cobwebbed. Grown mainly for their stiff rosette-forming leaves, they throw up sturdy heads of pink or red flowers. Late spring and summer. 4 ins.

Sidalcea (Greek Mallow), not unlike a miniature Hollyhock in pink and crimson, is easily grown in a not too cold garden. Aug. 2-4 ft.

Stachys lanata (Lamb's Ear), with attractive soft and silky grey leaves, the reddish-purple flowers covered with grey down being of secondary importance.

The most satisfactory of the silver-foliaged ground-cover plants, thriving on well-drained rather poor soil. July-Aug. 12-18 ins.

Thalictrum (Meadow Rue), with finely cut foliage not unlike the maidenhair and a host of fluffy purple or yellow flowers. 'Hewitt's Double' has panicles as light as thistledown. June-Aug. 2-5 ft.

Thymus (Thyme), with green, silver, yellow and variegated leaves and red, pink, or white flowers and mat-like foliage. *T. serpyllum*, the prostrate form, is ideal for filling the cracks between paving. June-Aug. 1-2 ins.

Tradescantia (Spiderwort), white, blue or purple three-petalled flowers with grass-like foliage. *T. virginiana*, a good dependable garden variety, is easy to please. June-Sept. 2 ft.

Trollius (Globe Flower), the yellow or gold giant Buttercup requiring a moist soil. April-June. 2 ft.

Verbascum, the June-flowering Mullein. The non-woolly types are the most desirable varieties but are uncertain in many areas. 5-6 ft.

Veronica is the Speedwell in blue, purple, pink and white. There are the alpine and dwarf shrubby Hebe types and the herbaceous varieties, ranging from 4-in. *V. teucrium amethystina* to the tall tapering spikes of *virginica alba*, 3½ ft. April-Aug. 6 ins-3 ft.

Vinca (Periwinkle), an excellent ground-cover plant. Single and double white, blue and purple flowers. Grows well on banks so long as it does not dry out. June-Sept. 6-10 ins.

Viola. The pansy and violet are members of this genus. The bedding Viola in a good range of colours is a useful perennial easy to propagate by spring cuttings. It demands a porous soil with a good humus content. May-Sept. 6 ins.

Pansies are not reliable perennials and are best renewed every year, and violets, although willing enough to grow in towns, present few flowers.

This list has been difficult to make and every gardener will cross out or write in a plant's name in this chapter, having rejoiced in a perennial that I have left out or suffered disappointment through one that I have mentioned.

16 Plants from Seed

It is difficult to generalize about towns for they are so different. Seeds will grow in London, Manchester, Liverpool and Birmingham, so long as they are given friable soil and get plenty of sun and air. Without these essentials, it is a losing battle which should not be attempted.

Seeds are the easiest and cheapest way of propagating many perennials, annuals and biennials for the mixed border. They are a great experience for the novice even if they do not thrive as they might.

Certain perennials such as the Aquilegia, Aster, Delphinium, Lupin, Phlox and Pyrethrum should be sown in the autumn in good situations, otherwise in the spring, and will require patience, for it may take three years before a plant reaches its zenith. Very fine seed is often best sown in boxes, seedlings pricked out when large enough to handle, and planted in the garden in the autumn.

Some seed is slow to germinate such as the Aquilegia, *Helleborus niger* (Christmas Rose) and the Polyanthus and may well take 6-12 months to germinate, unless sown immediately after collection.

Biennials such as the Wallflower and Canterbury Bell should be sown on a prepared seed-bed in April, May or June, moved on to a nursery-bed when requiring more elbow room, and planted in their flowering positions in September or October.

The Annuals

The annual is of particular interest to the townsman, for it gives exciting colour just when the spring flowerers have faded and the garden is beginning to look a trifle dull.

There are degrees of hardiness among the hardy annuals and the real toughs are the best suited for town life. I give a list of these at the end of the chapter. Meanwhile, I should like to mention a few that I have tested for many years and found town-worthy.

Every spring, I select a collection of five annuals for readers of the newspaper of which I am Gardening Editor and arrange for a well-known nurseryman to provide this for 2s. In 1966 over 11,000 readers grew these. I have had many, many letters of appreciation and not one complaint. Here are the big five. Godetia, Larkspur, Limnanthes (the Meadow Foam or the Poached Egg Plant), Marigold and Nasturtium (pink 'Cherry Rose'). When the spring weather is unfavourable, I substitute the Larkspur with Autumn Sunshine Sunflower, a particularly sturdy race of yellow, bronze and yellow flowerers growing to 4 ft.

Soil

Having decided where the seed is to be sown, the soil should be dug deep in the autumn allowing frost and wind to break it down during the winter. This will enable the gardener to hoe and rake to a fine tilth in the spring.

The bed must not be prepared when the soil is wet or sticky, and finally it must be lightly walked over and firmed to prevent air pockets.

A well-broken-down crumbly soil is ideal for seed sowing, with the top half-inch finely sieved. It must be damped before sowing.

When sowing in boxes, John Innes Seed Compost is a time-saver and readily available at the sundriesman. Here is an excellent recipe for those who wish to make a similar compost at home:

2 parts loam
1 part peat
1 part coarse sand
plus $1\frac{1}{2}$ ozs. superphosphate of lime and $\frac{3}{4}$ oz. ground
chalk or limestone per bushel.

After firming, the boxes should be lightly sprinkled with silver sand.

The Method of Raising Seed

Hardy annuals are usually sown in the garden where they are to flower. If sown in the autumn, they will flower earlier and, having survived the winter, they will probably give larger and more flowers than those sown in the spring. But in many towns, winter casualties are likely to be heavy. It is a good plan to split the seed packet and sow half in the autumn and half in the spring.

The half-hardy must be sown in February or March or in heat in the late winter and planted out in May or June. Some gardeners sow the hardy in the autumn and, leaving spaces for the half-hardy, sow these *in situ* in April or early May. This method only comes off when conditions are good.

A number of town gardeners have small greenhouses these days and possess self-contained propagators, and are able to send their seeds and seedlings off to a flying start.

Pre-warmed compost stored under glass a week or two before using hastens germination.

Meanwhile, many without glasshouse or frame have become exceedingly skilful in germinating seed in polythene bags on the window-sill in the kitchen with the help of a steaming kettle and, if they are lucky, a south-facing window.

Good light and a steady temperature are vital for indoor seed raising. A low steady temperature is infinitely preferable to a high one that falls dramatically at night.

Sowing

The compost should be watered before sowing and the seed sown while the compost is moist.

The gardener is usually advised to sow to a depth of roughly three times the seed's own diameter. As it is the besetting sin of the beginner to sow too deep and too thick, I would advise a rather lighter covering than this and when seeds are minute, mixing them with sand and shaking them out of a dice- or ludo-thrower as used in the nursery for playing snakes and ladders.

Seeds sown in the garden can either be sown in drills lined with damp peat, in stations (small pinches or heaps), or just scattered.

Seed sown is best marked for later identification by a sprinkling of sand.

Large seeds such as Nasturtiums should be sown 8-9 ins. apart.

Seed boxes should be covered with glass and brown paper; the soil being moist makes watering unnecessary; it is only too easy to wash or rot the seeds away.

Seed germination varies, Lilies being slow and Fritillarias even slower, taking a year or longer to sprout. However, most annuals show life in a week or ten days, if not with the same speed as mustard and cress.

Seedlings

Immediately the seeds in the box germinate, the glass and brown paper should be removed and the boxes placed where they can get good light and ventilation.

Seedlings in boxes usually begin to overcrowd themselves before they are large enough or the weather kind enough to plant them out.

These will have to be pricked out and, if the sun happens to be shining, will benefit by being shaded for a day or two.

A John Innes Potting Compost can either be bought or a mixture made for the purpose based on similar ingredients.

7 parts loam

3 parts peat

2 parts sharp or coarse sand

plus 4 ozs. John Innes Base Fertilizer and $\frac{3}{4}$ ozs. ground chalk or limestone per bushel.

The seedlings should be watered after transplanting and should be given plenty of ventilation once they are established. They must be hardened off and gradually acclimatized to the conditions they will have to meet when planted out in the garden.

Meanwhile, the seeds sown in the garden are likely to require thinning out and this should be done as soon as they are large enough to handle, otherwise they will become leggy and lose their vigour. If this should happen, they must be pinched back in the hope that they will recover the desired bushy branching habit.

Every care should be taken when thinning out not to disturb the fortunate seedling that is to be allowed to remain. A check at this stage of growth can be damaging.

Now before giving a general list of seeds likely to succeed in built-up areas, something should be said about the F1 hybrids and the Sweet Pea.

The F1 Hybrid

The F1 hybrid plays an important part in the modern seed catalogue. It is the result of the cross-mating of two distinct and specially-selected parent strains.

Although there are different methods of procedure, in the majority of cases the male pollen from a plant of one strain is crossed on the female part of a plant of another strain. The result is often a hybrid of a large colour range and great vigour, combined with a perfect evenness of habit.

Most of the F1 hybrids are the result of hand labour carried out in glasshouses, it often being necessary to keep the two parents apart in separate greenhouses. The sterilization of the female parents (the removal of pollen-bearing stamens before they produce pollen) is another operation that has to be done by hand.

It is not surprising with all the work involved that the F1 hybrid packet is more expensive than other strains and that it often contains fewer seeds than usual.

Cross-pollination has to be carried out every year as, unfortunately for the gardener, seed saved does not breed true to type.

The Petunia benefited strikingly from this technique; 'Cascade' and some of the doubles are enchanting. The Antirrhinum, Marigold, Nigella, Polyanthus and the little Double Daisy have all taken advantage of this exciting development. Meanwhile, F2's and other hybrids are on their way to us.

Sweet Peas

The Sweet Peas deserve a special note because of the new dwarf varieties.

No doubt the plant's many fans with open gardens in favourable counties will want and be able to grow magnificent 'White Ensign', lavender 'Leamington', bright carmine 'Carlotta' and other beauties as cordon plants. This is best done in the vegetable garden as the cordon strings and lines seldom fit in with border designs: bush plantings, however, are always an addition at the back of the herbaceous border and are far easier to grow.

But it is to the new dwarfs that the townsman should turn and there are now a number of them.

The dwarf bijou or bush, growing to 12-15 ins., with stems long enough for cutting, and the small flowered Little Sweethearts, 8-12 ins., thrive in containers of all kinds, including window-boxes, and require no staking. They form pleasant clumps and are extremely effective and their scent is superb.

Autumn sowings are not advised for those living in the centre of a town and February to May sowings are likely to be far more successful. Much will depend on the container being carefully crocked and the compost rich: well-rotted farmyard manure and leaf-mould make a good mixture.

Carmine 'Carlotta' and a few other varieties are extremely hard-skinned and these seeds should be slightly chipped opposite the eye with the sharpest of knives. The edge of a nail-file will fill the bill and is safer.

Hardy Annuals to Sow Outdoors

Alyssum
Calendula (Marigold)
Candytuft
Chrysanthemum carinatum (C. tricolor)
Clarkia
Collinsia bicolor
Convolvulus minor
Cornflower
Cynoglossum (can also be grown as a biennial)
Echium
Eschscholtzia
Godetia
Ionopsidium
Larkspur
Lavatera
Leptosiphon
Limnanthes douglasii
Linaria
Linum
Malope
Matthiola bicornis (Night-scented Stock)
Mignonette
Nasturtium
Nemophila insignis
Nigella or Love-in-a-Mist
Poppy
Salvia horminum
Silene armeria
Statice
Sweet Sultan
Sweet William (annual sorts)
Virginian Stock

17 Bedding Plants

The pony-drawn market cart loaded with bedding plants is a glorious early-summer sight. The bedders are brilliant little plants and June and July borders are often dull without them.

A cheap and satisfactory way of buying seedlings and pot plants is at a market or local nursery.

The gardener should choose the short, sturdy dark green and preferably named seedlings, and the bushy plants that have lost their look of the greenhouse. If he is interested in particular plants such as the Geranium or silver-foliaged plants, he should, if possible, visit a specialist nurseryman.

Old-time geometrical-pattern carpet bedding is completely out of fashion, and the town gardener has learnt the value of relieving the greenery here and there with a splash of Geraniums or a block of massed Lobelias, but keeping the red and blue apart.

Flatness, which can be boring, may be broken with tall plants or standards of heliotrope Plumbago or Fuchsia, and colour schemes that break monotony are legion.

Meanwhile, whatever the plant, the beds must be well dug and prepared and generously fed with manure or, failing this, a reputable fertilizer. Summer bedding should not be planted until the third week in May, otherwise, there is always the danger of being defeated by a late frost.

All plants should be given a thorough watering the day before they are to be bedded out. They should be firmly planted, using fingers rather than the butt of the trowel, which is best left to the professional.

Geraniums

The Pelargonium, more commonly known as the Geranium, is one of the most widely planted of bedding plants.

The single zonal geraniums all with five petals have a luminous quality and florets of 2-2½ ins. in diameter, while the double are handsome, with multi-petal flowers and circular markings on their scalloped leaves.

Scarlet 'Paul Crampel' and partially semi-double scarlet 'Gustave Emich', the Buckingham Palace Geranium, are great performers, but have been over-exposed during the last years. I should like to see more of 'Orangesonne', a brilliant orange of excellent habit, 'Vera Dillon', a single magenta, soft satin-pink 'Mrs Lawrence', and vivid vermilion 'Irene'.

The ivy-leaved varieties are ideal for tubs, urns, and hanging baskets. They are in lovely colours with a fuller range of mauves than the zonals. Imperial 'La France', with its upper petals feathered white and peony purple, is one of the many remarkably beautiful varieties.

Now that Geraniums have returned to popularity, ornamental or variegated leaf varieties are once again available. Silvery white and green 'Flower of Spring', golden-leaved 'Crystal Palace Gem', golden tricolour 'Mrs Pollock', and the most brilliant of all tricolours, 'Mrs Henry Cox', with bronze, red and cream-yellow variegations, are to be had from a number of Geranium specialists.

I am particularly pleased that the miniatures have been welcomed back for they are a fascinating group, some with large, almost black flowers that all but over-balance the small plant. The miniature with fancy-leaved variations seldom exceeds 8 ins.

Culture

Geraniums need the sun and a good summer to be at their best. They are not hardy and must be brought inside before there is any danger of frost and I have just lost a treasured plant of 'L'Elegante' in my kitchen as a result of the temperature falling below 40°F.

Pot plants should be watered with care. They can survive drought for several months, but damp soggy soil is fast to kill. The plants should be watered only to avoid desert-dryness through the winter.

The Geranium enjoys good fare but the fertilizer given must be well-balanced. Should it contain too much nitrogen, then the plants will grow large and leafy and present few flowers. John Innes Compost No. 2 or 3 is suitable for pots and small urns, while a good heavy loam of a closer consistency can be used for window-boxes and larger containers.

When repotting, plant firmly, underpotting rather than over-potting as the Geranium seldom flowers until its roots have reached the side of the pot.

Leaf-shedding is customary after the disturbance of repotting, and the yellowing leaves should be removed.

Cuttings are best taken from August to October. Firm shoots 3-4 ins. long, cleanly cut just below the third or fourth joints, avoiding sappy stems, should be inserted at the side of a pot. Hormone Rooting Powder encourages striking and cuttings should be ready to be potted up singly by February.

Useful Bedding Plants

Abutilon	1½-5 ft.	Pink, including the Hedde-	
Ageratum	6-18 ins.	wigii varieties)	9-12 ins.
Antirrhinum (Snap-		Dahlia (including dwarf	
dragon)	12-18 ins.	varieties)	1½-3 ft.
Asters	8-15 ins.	Echeveria (Cotyledon)	9-12 ins.
Begonia (tuberous and		Eucalyptus	from 3 ft.
fibrous-rooted)	8-12 ins.	Fuchsia	1-2 ft.
Bellis (Daisy)	6-8 ins.	Geranium (ivy-leaved and	
Calceolaria	12 ins.	zonal varieties)	6-18 ins.
Canna	3 ft.	Heliotrope (Cherry Pie)	1-3 ft.
Celosia (Cock's Comb)	18 ins.	Impatiens (Busy Lizzie)	6 ins.
Centaurea	18 ins.	Lobelia	12 ins.
Cerastium tomentosum		Marguerite (Paris Daisy)	1-2 ft.
(Snow-in-Summer)	6 ins.	Matricaria	12 ins.
Chrysanthemum	2-3 ft.	Mimulus (Musk)	6 ins.
Cineraria maritima	6-12 ins.	Myosotis (Forget-me-not)	6 ins.
Coleus	18 ins.	Nicotiana (including	
Dianthus chinensis (Annual		dwarf varieties)	2-3 ft.

Pansy	6 ins.	Salvia (Clary)	2 ft.
Penstemon (annual		Stocks, Ten-Week	12 ins.
varieties)	1-2 ft.	Verbena	9 ins.
Petunia	12 ins.	Viola	6 ins.
Phlox drummondii	12 ins.	Wallflower	12 ins.
Polyanthus	8 ins.	Zinnia	1-2 ft.

18 Roses

The rose has been Britain's best-loved flower since the twelfth century. Fortunately, it is easy to grow and cheap. Comfortably planted in the winter, it can be relied upon to flower the following summer.

As the flamboyant rose-grower Harry Wheatcroft often remarks, 'A good heart and a bucket of muck is all that is needed.' But there are other essential requirements not always available in a town—air and sun.

Shut in by walls or planted under trees, competing with hungry roots and suffering from the drip of overhanging branches and semi-shade, the rose can only give a very poor performance.

Some of our best roses come from small gardens where the plant enjoys the enthusiastic and individual attention of the gardener, and the by-passes are often flower shows in themselves.

Culture

Roses seem to grow best when they are in beds or borders on their own, which simplifies their care. A pattern of grouped varieties, three or four of a kind, comes off far better than a bed of mixed colour.

Under-planting is allowed, and spring bulbs, Pinks or Violas relieve a rose-bed's bareness.

Shrub and standard roses will be found a great addition to the herbaceous border while the hybrid climbers are enchanting on a wall. Ramblers will willingly cascade over pillars, posts and pergolas, and the Sweet Briars make a perfect scented hedge.

Roses can be planted from the end of October until the end of March. If the ground is frozen, sticky or sodden, the roses should be heeled in under the shelter of a hedge. This is preferable to keeping them in the spare room. The right moment for permanent planting is when the weather is 'open' and the soil is easy to handle.

The belief that clay soil is the one and only diet for roses has been exploded. Broken-up clay certainly provides some of our best roses, but a determined gardener on ordinary soil who is willing to fork in a generous amount of farmyard manure often grows some of the finest blooms.

If farmyard manure is not available, home-made compost, peat or hop-manure plus a sprinkling of bonemeal, can be substituted. Old turf chopped up and buried below the top spit is also helpful. Such additions to heavy land will break up the clay, enable light soil to retain moisture, while offsetting any excess of lime, when on chalk.

It is important to prepare the ground well before planting. After-care, however considerate, does not compensate for a poor start. It is in the top twelve inches of soil that the rose feeds by means of its fibrous roots. The rosarian should never bury his treasure, nor manure much deeper.

Planting

A plant that has dried out on the journey from the nursery should be soaked or 'puddled' in a bucket of soil and water. If the mud-porridge sticks to the roots, so much the better.

A hole of 15-16 ins. wide and 8 ins. deep should then be dug. 'Don't put a guinea plant in a sixpenny hole,' is the veteran's maxim.

The bushes should be planted about 18 ins. apart in staggered rows, and stationed at least 12 ins. away from the edge of the bed. Experts tell us to spread the rose roots out horizontally all the way round. As the roots often grow one way only, this may well be an impossibility and the best one can do is to hold the rose at the side of the hole and spread the roots out the way they dictate.

If the novice is doubtful as to the right depth for planting, he can study the soil mark on the stem and set out to plant up to that level, remembering that plants have a habit of sinking to a slightly lower level.

Deep planting is a bad fault and must be guarded against, while firm planting is a golden rule, bringing the soil into close contact with the roots. We are told by rosarians that it is impossible to plant a rose too firmly.

Finally, when tidying up, loosen the top inch of soil so that the rain can drain down to the roots. If, as often happens, a hard frost lifts the newly-planted roses, they should be trodden back in place when the weather breaks.

Pruning

This operation is necessary in order to keep the rose-bush nicely shaped and to encourage it to flower on young wood, which gives the best blooms.

There are different opinions about the wisdom of light or hard pruning and a constant battle among rosarians as to the right time to do this work. The wise gardener will avoid argument and dogmatism.

Meanwhile, the harder the pruning, the larger but fewer the blooms. The most successful growers seem in favour of pruning moderately to hard in early March. But there are those who feel strongly that December to January is a better time. It is noticeable that hard cutting back, other than for the elderly rose that is deteriorating, is not as fashionable as it was.

Some roses require pruning more than others, and a handbook, *The Cultivation of the Rose*, is published by the Royal National Rose Society and is available to members.

Weak or unhealthy growth can be cut out at any time. Gardeners will find secateurs easier to handle than a knife, provided they are kept sharp. Notes on pruning the different types of roses will be found under each heading.

Aphids

Greenfly is the rose's constant enemy, but if the plants are healthy and the gardener is on the alert before the hosts arrive, the invader can be controlled.

HETP is a quick killer; Nicotine deadly on warm days and Derris slow but fairly sure. One insecticide treatment is unlikely to settle the matter for the whole summer.

Greenfly are mightily prolific: a watchful eye and immediate action is the answer and preventive sprays are always worthwhile.

Rose Sickness

Blackspot is a common fungus disease particularly prevalent during a wet summer, black or purple specks appearing on mature leaves.

If the infection is severe, foliage is shed as early as June, weakening the plant, and new leaves are likely to be attacked by mildew.

Diseased stems and twigs and leaves must be carefully collected and burned and the plant sprayed with a colloidal copper white oil emulsion such as Captan.

Blackspot is less prevalent in densely populated areas than in the open country, possibly due to the sulphurous acid in the atmosphere of built-up and industrial areas having an inhibiting effect on the fungus.

Mildew is the commonest rose disease and easily distinguished, the leaves and stems becoming white as if dusted with white powder. One of the first symptoms is the white-grey spots that arrive on the young leaves, which, spreading rapidly, turn a reddish colour. The young growth then becomes dwarfed and misshapen and damaged leaves fall.

Enclosed town conditions are apt to encourage mildew during damp periods and susceptible varieties such as 'Crimson Glory' should not be planted in airless gardens.

Mildew is the easiest disease to treat, lying as it does on the surface of the leaves and stems. Karathane, another colloidal copper white oil emulsion, will also be found an effective control if used early in the season.

Rust is an unaccountable disease that appears from time to time, usually in areas where there are early and heavy dews. The disease first shows itself as small rust-coloured swellings on the under surface of the leaf.

No entirely satisfactory treatment has yet been found for rust, but all infected leaves must be collected and burnt. The soil beneath the infected plant should be turned over and the plant sprayed with Thiram or a colloidal cupreous oxide oil emulsion, giving particular attention to the undersides of the leaves.

Chlorosis, the loss of green colouring matter in foliage and consequent yellowing, may be the result of overwatering, unsatisfactory drainage, lack of light, or a condition due to iron deficiency. Iron chelates marketed as Sequestrene, soluble in water, should be applied to the soil. At a suitably low strength, this product can also be used as a foliage spray.

Suckers

The gardener must beware of suckers. These usually come from below ground and should be pulled away as soon as possible. The novice may have difficulty in deciding whether a new growth is an unwanted sucker or a desirable new shoot.

Most cultivated rose shoots have five leaflets and there is no truth in the saying that 'any growth that carries leaves having more than five leaflets is a sucker'. The only way of finding out whether the growth is a sucker or not is to trace it back to its source; if it is found to come from below the union or point of budding, then it is a sucker and should be pulled away.

At the Royal National Rose Society's Trial Gardens at St Albans, Hertfordshire, suckers are removed with a daisy-grubber.

Manures and Fertilizers

All roses require generous feeding. An annual 2-in. mulch of home-made compost, plus animal manure is advised. If the gardener has no compost heap, granulated peat can be used in its place, applying a layer about 1-2 ins. thick.

Soils vary and therefore require different treatments, but organic manures are generally helpful, while chemical fertilizers are helpful in supplying any special deficiency.

Reputable chemical fertilizers are useful, but they do not replace the bulky organic manures which are so essential.

Many showmen and successful gardeners give a feed of John Innes Base after pruning and again a reputable rose fertilizer such as Humber fish manure (Eclipse) after the first flush. Enthusiasts follow-up with a third feed, possibly of dried blood at the rate of 2-3 ozs. per square yard, in July after the second flush. Here a halt must be called, otherwise soft growth will be encouraged that will not ripen.

Meanwhile, a completely soluble fertilizer once a fortnight during May and once a week in June works wonders.

Mulching and General Care

Mulching entails the placing of organic matter over the surface ground in order to conserve the moisture in the soil from the hot sun and drying winds. It also feeds the plant.

Few gardeners have enough mulching material to go round all their plants. However, grass cuttings (no more than an inch thick and free from any form of weedkiller), sawdust, semi-rotted stable manure, straw, dead leaves and compost all serve the purpose.

The mulch should be moist and placed round the plant after it has been watered or following a rainfall.

Mulching generally has the happy result of keeping down the weeds.

Care must be taken when raking or forking not to disturb the rose's fine roots that are close to the surface. Well-rotted manure can be placed round the base of the tree, the layer being lightly covered with soil and allowed to rot down at its own pace.

When watering, real soakings should be given rather than dribs and drabs that merely bring roots to the top soil. A syringing each evening will freshen the foliage.

The Various Types of Roses

The Hybrid Tea

This is a popular bush rose of some 2-4 ft. Its first flush of flowers is normally in June, after which it flowers intermittently until September when it has a further full crop.

The flower usually has a shapely pointed centre and a rich scent. The colour range is large but does not yet include a true blue, although 'Sterling Silver', 'Blue Moon' and others are on their way towards it.

When it comes to pruning, the hybrid tea should be pruned harder than the floribunda, the aim being an open cup-shaped bush. The first year, the bush should be pruned to a plump eye, pointing outwards four eyes from the base.

133

Subsequent years, all weak twiggy growths and the previous year's ripened growth should be reduced to about half its length. All stems that are damaged and of soft unripe wood should be removed at their base. The pruning cut should be clean, sloping, and about a quarter of an inch above a plump but dormant eye.

Light pruning is advised for certain varieties, leaving the previous year's ripe growth intact. There are gardeners who reap good results from allowing their plant to grow almost unpruned: the large plant that results will need extra feeding. All decadent wood must be cut away, two or three eyes from the base.

Varieties. Not all roses have the vigour to stand up to town life; many, making only weak growth, rapidly deteriorate. The virtues to be looked for when choosing roses for a town garden are strength, hardiness, disease-resistance, and dependability of colour. They should not be of too delicate a shade in areas where they are likely to be soiled by smog or grimy atmosphere. Few roses have all town qualities—perhaps only one, 'Peace'. (Alas, there are fears that this magnificent performer is now on the decline.)

However, a good word should be put in for 'Betty Uprichard' (salmon); 'Ernest H. Morse' (crimson); 'Fragrant Cloud' (dusky scarlet); 'Frau Karl Druschki' (white); 'Gail Borden' (pink and yellow); 'Grand'mère Jenny' (yellow and pink); 'Lady Sylvia' (rose-pink); 'Madame Butterfly' (pink-apricot and gold); 'Mrs Sam McGredy' (pink with orange); 'Ophelia' (blush) and 'President Herbert Hoover' (pink with yellow).

Floribundas

The floribunda is a descendant of the polyantha and the flowers come in handsome clusters. Some varieties such as 'Paddy McGredy' carry flowers almost as large as the hybrid tea.

Hardy and constantly in flower, the floribunda is less vulnerable to disease and pest than the hybrid tea and is an excellent bedding plant.

Light pruning will produce early flowers, and hard pruning later blooms and desirable new growth. During the first year, bushes should be cut down to about six inches from the ground;

subsequently, the one-year-old wood should be only lightly pruned and the older wood moderately hard.

Varieties. The floribunda varieties are legion. The following lead the way and usually give satisfaction even in difficult areas: 'Iceberg' (white); 'Joybells' (rich pink-salmon—thorny but tough); 'Olala' (crimson); 'Paprika' (dusky scarlet); 'Queen Elizabeth' (rose-pink); 'Red Dandy' (crimson-scarlet) and 'Vera Dalton' (rose-pink).

Climbers

It is often said that the hybrid climber is not worth the space it occupies on the wall. So far as climbing 'Peace' is concerned, this is true. Although it does well in Spain and the South of France, it is notorious as a non-flowerer in this country and several nurserymen are dropping this rose from their lists. It is best dug up and discarded.

But roses such as veterans pink 'Caroline Testout' and red 'Étoile de Hollande' make up for the ungenerous flowerers.

Damaged and decadent wood should be thinned out in February and the flowering laterals of the previous year shortened to two eyes.

The main stems of climbing hybrids must not be cut back severely the first year, otherwise they may revert to bush form. 'Mermaid', being slow to establish itself, requires no pruning other than to keep it in place.

Varieties. 'Danse du Feu' (dusky-scarlet); 'Golden Showers' (clear yellow); 'New Dawn' (blush) and 'Zéphirine Drouhin' (deep pink—thornless).

Ramblers

These small-flowered roses present large, showy clusters of bloom during June or July.

'Dorothy Perkins' is still one of the most popular of the group, with 'American Pillar' close on her heels, while Wichuraiana 'Albertine' is strong and glorious.

Pruning for the rambler: all flowering wood can be cut back to ground level once the bloom is over and replaced by young stout growth.

Pruning is simplified by loosening all ties, laying the stems on the ground and operating from there.

New growth must then be trained in, as it is upon this that the plant will flower the following year.

Polyantha Pompoms

The dwarf polys are compact and have small flowers the summer through.

The dwarfs require moderate to hard pruning. Stems should be cut back (half their length) to an outward-pointing eye, while dismissing old wood that is not producing sturdy shoots.

Varieties. 'Cameo' (salmon-pink); 'Coral Cluster' (rich coral-pink); 'Little Dorrit' (coral-salmon) and 'Paul Crampel' (orange-scarlet) lead the way.

Shrub and Rose Species—including the Old-fashioned Roses

There are town gardeners who do not consider the species altogether practical for cities, since they take up a lot of room and give but one performance. But old and modern roses cannot be fairly compared and it would be dreadful to leave out the superb old-fashioned and other shrub roses, for they have a distinction that the contemporary varieties do not possess.

Were there ever more romantic flowers than deliciously-scented apple-blossom Bourbon 'Madame Pierre Oger'; striped and splashed pink-purple 'Commandant Beaurepaire', or ivory camellia-like 'Boule de Neige' that is heavily loaded with scent?

Among the Gallicas, purple-crimson 'Charles de Mills', with its amazing folds and quarterings of the greatest richness; pale pink striped carmine 'Georges Vibert'; and carmine and pale pink striped on white 'Rosa Mundi', the gayest and largest of the striped roses.

My pick of the Damasks is 'Celsiana' in pure dog-rose pink. These are flowers that have inspired the painters and poets and I hope will do the same for the town gardener.

The scented perpetual-flowering Musks have a good bushy habit, growing to four or five feet, and creamy-pink 'Penelope' will make an interesting feature at the back of the border with its attractive grey foliage decked in autumn with coral-pink hips.

Then there are the spinosissima hybrids, 'Frühlingsgold' and others, the Lord Penzance Briars, and the Moss roses, including *Rosa centifolia muscosa*, the heavenly pink moss rose which opens to disclose fascinating button eyes and which is unsurpassed since its arrival in 1727.

I end my eulogy of the old roses with a 1927 hybrid, the beautiful white 'Nevada', said to be a hybrid of *R. moyesii*, with arching, almost thornless branches reaching to some six or seven feet, and nearly five-inch almost single flowers with striking rich golden stamens.

I hope I have whetted the reader's appetite sufficiently for him to buy at least this one rose, for it is a great addition to a garden.

The care of these roses is not heavy work; they should be shaped rather than pruned in order to keep them within their allotted space.

Admittedly, the pernickety gardener may find the shrubs a trifle untidy, but if during the first years he removes the twiggy, unsatisfactory growths and later dismisses old spent wood when sprucing up the border in the winter, all should be well.

From time to time shoots can be shortened to within half a dozen buds in the spring. Deadheading is necessary as the flat flowers hold the water and brown and wet deadheads rob later buds and blooms of their freshness.

Miniature Roses

Few miniatures are as perfect as the 6-12 ins. high roses. They are hardy, but should be given a well-drained soil and must not be allowed to dry out.

Humus, leaf-mould and compost is a suitable diet. Pruning consists in the removal of poor, unripe wood.

Varieties. 'Baby Masquerade' (yellow and red); 'Pour Toi' (white tinted yellow at base); and 'Rosina' (sunflower yellow).

Summing-up

The rose is a valuable investment that will last ten years or more. Gardeners sometimes complain that the modern rose has lost its fragrance. They should put their noses into 'Fragrant Cloud', 'Golden Melody', 'Red Ensign'; black-red climber 'Guinée' or 'Premier Bal'.

The lists that follow are published by kind permission of the Royal National Rose Society.

Most Fragrant Hybrid Tea Roses

André le Troquer
Betty Uprichard
Blue Moon
Bond Street
Charles Mallerin
Christopher Stone
Chrysler Imperial
Crimson Glory
Diorama
Eden Rose
Elsa Arnot
Ena Harkness
Ernest H. Morse
Fragrant Cloud
Golden Melody
Grace de Monaco
Hector Deane
Hugh Dickson
Josephine Bruce
June Park
Konrad Adenauer
Lady Seton

Lady Sylvia
Mme Butterfly
Monique
My Choice
Ophelia
Papa Meilland
Pink Perfume
Polly
President Herbert Hoover
Prima Ballerina
Red Devil
Rubaiyat
Shot Silk
Signora
Silver Lining
Sterling Silver
Super Star
Sutter's Gold
Teenager
The Doctor
Wendy Cussons
Westminster

Beginners' Roses

Hardy and vigorous hybrid tea roses that are likely to succeed in industrial areas and other unfavourable positions.

White
Frau Karl Druschki

Cream, Pale Orange and Flesh
Anne Watkins
Ophelia
Polly

Deep Pink
Eden Rose
Hector Deane
Pink Favourite
Prima Ballerina
Sarah Arnot
South Seas

Pink and Yellow Blends
Chicago Peace
Gail Borden
My Choice
President Herbert Hoover
Teenager

Orange, Pink and Flame Blends
Bayadère
Mojave
Signora

Orange, Shaded Yellow
Diorama
Doreen

Vermilion and Coral Salmon
Mischief
Super Star

Bicolours
Grand Gala (scarlet and silver)
Ideal Home (pink and silver)
Kronenbourg (scarlet and gold, deepening to purple)
Piccadilly (scarlet and gold)

Light Pink
Anne Letts
Grace de Monaco
Lady Sylvia
Caroline Testout
Margaret
Monique
Rose Gaujard (pink and silver)
Stella (pink and cream)

Salmon, Carmine, Cerise and Light Red
Bacchus
Betty Uprichard
Montezuma
Wendy Cussons

Geranium Red
Allegro
Fragrant Cloud
Lucy Cramphorn

Deep Scarlet to Deep Crimson
Ena Harkness
Hugh Dickson
Josephine Bruce
Karl Herbst
Milord
Uncle Walter

Yellow and Yellow tinted Pink
Buccaneer
Gold Crown
Grand'mère Jenny
Grandpa Dickson
Peace
Spek's Yellow
Sutter's Gold

Most of the floribunda roses are also suitable.

Roses for Pillars

Climbers of moderate vigour suitable for training on poles or pillars up to 8 ft in height. Repeat flowering except where stated.

Aloha
Altissimo
Casino
Chaplin's Pink Climber (summer-flowering only)
Copenhagen
Coral Dawn
Danse du Feu
Dortmund
Etude
Fashion (Clg.)
Golden Dawn (Clg.) (summer-flowering only)
Goldilocks (Clg.)
Hamburger Phoenix
Handel
Joseph's Coat
Kathleen Harrop

Korona (Clg.)
Maigold
Masquerade (Clg.)
Meg
Mme Isaac Pereire
New Dawn
Parade
Parkdirektor Riggers
Paul's Lemon Pillar (summer-flowering only)
Paul's Scarlet Climber (summer-flowering only)
Pink Perpétue
Reveil Dijonnais
Ritter von Barmstede
Schoolgirl
Soldier Boy
Zéphirine Drouhin

These varieties are also suitable for hedges, if trained horizontally and tied to stakes when necessary.

ROSES

Roses for Arches and Pergolas
Summer-flowering only

Albertine
American Pillar
Chaplin's Pink Climber
Crimson Conquest
Crimson Shower
Dorothy Perkins
Dr W. Van Fleet
Easlea's Golden Rambler
Emily Gray

Excelsa
François Juranville
Mme Grégoire Staechelin
Mary Wallace
Minnehaha
Paul's Scarlet Climber
Sanders' White
Veilchenblau

Most of the vigorous climbing hybrid tea sports are also suitable, but they have stouter wood which makes them less graceful and tractable.

Shrubs and Hedges

Repeat-flowering roses for growing as shrubs or hedges of 4 ft or over. For hedges, plant not more than 3 ft apart.

Blanc double de Coubert
Chicago Peace
Chinatown
Cornelia
Dorothy Wheatcroft
Eden Rose
Elmshorn
Erfurt
Felicia
Frau Dagmar Hastrup
Grüss an Teplitz
Heidelberg
Kassel
Lady Sonia
Lavender Lassie

Moonlight
Nymphenburg
Peace
Penelope
Prosperity
Queen Elizabeth
R. rugosa alba
Rose Gaujard
Roseraie de l'Hay
Sarah Van Fleet
Schneezwerg
Sparrieshoop
Uncle Walter
Wilhelm
Will Scarlett

Roses for Walls

For walls facing East, North or North-East

Allen Chandler	Mme Alfred Carrière
Conrad F. Meyer	Caroline Testout (Clg.)
Danse du Feu	Mme Grégoire Staechelin
Felicité et Perpétue	Maigold
Gloire de Dijon	Nova Zembla
Grüss an Teplitz	Parkdirektor Riggers
Guinée	Paul's Lemon Pillar
Hugh Dickson	Soldier Boy

For walls facing South or West

Elegance	Mme Edouard Herriot (Clg.)
Ena Harkness (Clg.)	Mme Henri Guillot (Clg.)
Etoile de Hollande (Clg.)	Meg
Golden Dawn (Clg.)	Mermaid
Goldilocks (Clg.)	Mrs Sam McGredy (Clg.)
Lady Hillingdon (Clg.)	Royal Gold
Lady Sylvia (Clg.)	Shot Silk (Clg.)

and most other climbing sports of the hybrid teas.

The varieties given in the previous selection for east, north and north-east walls are also suitable for a south or west wall.

It should be noted that the Wichuraiana ramblers are *not* suitable for training on walls.

Roses for covering stumps, steep banks and as ground cover

Max Graf	R. *paulii*
R. '*Macrantha*' (of gardens)	R. *wichuraiana*

Also all the ramblers of lax growth, especially Crimson Shower, Dorothy Perkins, Excelsa, François Juranville, Minnehaha, Sanders' White and Veilchenblau.

19 Grey-foliaged Plants

Touches of white and grey are extremely effective in a garden but few of the ever-greys can be treated as perennials in difficult towns, disliking as they do clogging dirt, fog and smog, against which it is almost impossible to protect them.

Sun is essential to the white-and grey-leaved groups, for the hairs that create their white and grey appearance only come into being in order to protect the plant against the dry and scorching effect of the sun.

Gardeners living in coastal towns should grow—and do well with—the silver-foliaged plants, for they enjoy the bright light and the majority seem to have no objection to salty spray.

But to the unfortunates who live in a heavily-polluted atmosphere I can offer little hope of growing permanent plants, although here are some of the toughest of the greys for the courageous.

Anaphalis nubigena, with grey leaves and clusters of pearly immortelle flowers. Aug. 8 ins.

A. triplinervis, a little larger and bolder than *nubigena*, and a remarkably tidy plant. Aug. 12 ins.

Artemisia absinthium 'Lambrook Silver', an impressive cascading plant with silver leaves and mimosa-like flowers. July. Plumes 3 ft. Tussocks 18 ins.

A. arborescens, a shimmering silver plant for the back of the border, a perfect companion for the delphinium. July. 3 ft.

A. schmidtii nana, a silky plant for the front of the border with silver cushions that turn red in autumn. July.

Santolina chamaecyparissus serratifolia, with feathery foliage. Yellow flowers with an unfortunate scent. July. 2½ ft.

The greys lose much of their charm if they are not lit up here and there with the white-foliaged. So, as a compromise, I suggest that the plants in the above list are interplanted with a few of the more tender whites to be treated as annuals.

The following four are delightful, but they require sun, an open position and clean air to be long-lived.

Gazania 'Silver Beauty' covers the ground with distinguished white-felted leaves but is tender. The yellow flowers with black centres are better pinched out so that all strength goes to the plant.

Helichrysum petiolatum also has white-felted foliage. The insignificant flowers are best removed for the sake of the plant's virility. 7 ins.

Senecio 'White Diamond', with flat flower-heads and diamond-shaped leaves: probably the whitest of the group. July. 2 ft.

Stachys lanata, already given in my list of perennials. 12 ins.

To a pocket-handkerchief garden and a gardener with time and a little money to spare, they are invaluable.

A minute London garden in Cadogan Place

A mews garden in St Marylebone designed by John Brookes

Interesting screen wall units in a garden in Chelsea
designed by A. du Gard Pasley

20 Bulbs

Bulbs are the town gardener's best friend so long as he wisely buys and obeys the few essential rules.

All bulbs are best bought from a bulb specialist, as their performance will reflect the preparation and treatment given the previous year: bargain offers made late in the season are responsible for many disappointments.

Healthy bulbs are fairly easily distinguished—they should be firm and weighty.

If the bulb is in good order, then the embryo bloom is safely tucked away in its centre; failing this, a magician—much less a gardener—cannot make it flower in the spring.

The rules are few, but good drainage is essential. Organic matter in the shape of good compost, peat, leaf-mould, or failing these, hop-manure is a suitable diet, plus bonemeal. Animal manure must only be used if almost completely rotted.

A sprinkling of silver sand at the base of the bulb is helpful, particularly on heavy soil.

The trowel is the best tool for planting the large bulbs, while a flat-bottomed dibber or your fingers are suitable for the small ones. The bulbs must sit securely at the bottom of the hole, and air-pockets must be avoided.

The planting depth for bulbs depends a little on soil and should be slightly deeper on very light ground. If in doubt, the beginner should measure the bulb from base to shoulder and plant at double this measurement.

Bulbs should be planted as soon as possible after arrival, for if left in their bags, even for a short period, they deteriorate.

Hyacinths

The Hyacinth is a first-rate tub, window-box, balcony, urn, court-yard or back-door plant, placed where its fresh and delicious scent can be captured and appreciated.

Its strong stem and loaded truss of bell-shaped flowers make it a formal plant. The medium-sized bulb is the best for the garden, the top-sized often toppling in the wind.

This is a wonderfully dependable bulb, and when bought from a reputable source will seldom default. It should be planted in a good loam in September or October about 4 ins. deep. On heavy soil, the basal plate should sit on a pinch of silver sand.

There is a bedding hyacinth list that should be consulted.

Navy-blue 'Ostara' and white 'L'Innocence' are early and easy; the yellow varieties are just a little temperamental and should be found a favoured place; and the Roman group is more delicate but the most beautiful of them all.

Daffodils

There are now, according to the Royal Horticultural Society, nine divisions of Narcissus, or in common English, Daffodils. Among them, the trumpets, large and small-cupped, doubles, tazettas, jonquils, bunch-flowered and others.

They should be planted during the last two weeks of September; if left until after early October, they are likely to suffer some deterioration in foliage if not in flower.

They should be planted 5-7 ins. or so apart, 5 ins. deep on heavy, 6 ins. deep on light soil. They can be left undisturbed for three years, when they should be lifted in July and the small offsets detached and replanted separately.

Daffodils are excellent for naturalizing if the gardener is prepared to let the foliage die right down before using the scythe or mower. If the leaves are cut back before June the bulb is unable to send nourishment back to the storeroom, with the result that the following spring's performance will be much poorer.

When it comes to deciding upon varieties, there is a superabundance of choice.

Conservative gardeners who insist on their Daffodils being golden-yellow with trumpets, will find plenty of these in the bulb-man's catalogue at 1s. 6d. to 2s. each, while Mrs Lionel Richardson of Waterford, Ireland, the leading daffodil breeder of the world, can supply show breeder's Narcissus at £25 each upwards.

The white Daffodils have already caught the public eye and now the adventurous are embarking upon the new exciting rose and apricot tints known as the pinks. My choice remains white trumpet 'Cantatrice' of exquisite texture and perfect grace and I am glad to say it is now comparatively cheap.

Tulips

The Tulips are a splendid addition to the town garden; they have colour and diversity, and, chosen with care, will flower from early March until June.

Their cultivation is simple. They are best planted in October, there being a risk of disease if planted earlier. If possible, a fresh place should be found for the bulbs each year as this minimizes the spreading of the dreaded Fire Disease.

A sunny, well-drained position and light rich loam suits the Tulip. The bulbs should be placed 4-5 ins. deep and shallow planting avoided.

If left for a second year, the flowers will generally be reduced in size, while some will fail to bloom altogether. However, the small bulblets, if carefully nursed, may flower the following season.

Here is but a taste from the tremendous Tulip list.

The curtain goes up in late March or April with the early singles to flower with the Daffodils. They are short-stemmed but sturdy and in gay colours.

The double Tulips follow on in April and their peony-like blooms are appreciated for their long-lasting quality and their fascinating habit of flinging themselves open to the sun.

The Cottage Tulips arrive in May, and their symmetrical heads in soft colours make them light and elegant.

The Triumphs are a new race and a cross between the singles, earlies and Darwins. They flower in April, stay until May, and are vigorous and strong. A good choice for an exposed or unpromising position and for the town.

The Parrot Tulips are the Bohemian branch of the family, with laciniated petals that always attract attention. A bulb that demands a special sheltered place.

The Lily-flowered Tulips with their superb reflex habit are to my mind, the most beautiful of them all. 'China Pink' with Cambridge blue Forget-me-nots in the offing is a lovely planting.

The Viridiflora or Green Tulips, flowering in mid-May, have their inevitable green 'blaze' or marking, which makes them different from all the Tulips we have known in the past and the beloved of the flower arranger. 'Hummingbird', with its rather square head on a sturdy stem with a wide 'blaze' of orchid green turning to Chinese yellow at the edges, and 'Artist', with its pointed petals changing from green to purple, rose and apricot, are unique.

The Multiflora Tulips, May branch-flowering newcomers, have also caused something of a sensation, with three to six flower heads on a stem.

The Darwin remains the formal King of the Tulips, and great advance has been made in their stately bearing and richness of colour.

Lastly, there are the distinguished species for the connoisseur, *T. clusiana*, the Lady Tulip, *T. kaufmanniana*, the enchanting Water-lily Tulip, cream and carmine, and *Tulipa fosteriana* hybrids such as dashing 'Madame Lefeber' or 'Red Emperor', of an oriental scarlet of such brilliance that the onlooker is forced to blink.

I have given but a taste of the Tulips, leaving the comprehensive bulb catalogues to whet the appetite further.

Crocus and other small bulbs

The large-flowered Dutch crocus are tough little bulbs that, once well-planted, will increase rapidly and look after themselves.

'Joan of Arc', cream-white with a lavender flush, is particularly beautiful, but there is a long list to choose from and the Dutch crocus will be found good value for money.

The species are smaller and, flowering in late February, a few weeks earlier than the Dutch, are more carefully sculptured and distinguished in form and colouring than the Dutch and should be allotted a privileged place.

'Chrysanthus E. A. Bowles', golden-ochre, with dark grey mark-

ings at the base of the petals and bronze throat with orange stig-
mata, is a masterpiece that should not be missed.

The Crocus likes a leaf-mould mixture, and should be planted
3 ins. deep in August or September.

The winter-flowering buttercup, Winter Aconite, with its green
Toby collar, and the Snowdrop, are the first to flower in the spring,
but the blue Scillas that spread so splendidly if left undisturbed
and the blue Grape Hyacinths are not far behind them.

Deep violet *Iris reticulata* blotched yellow, has many admirers,
but the dwarf species, yellow *I. danfordiae* and flax-blue *I. histrioides* with golden crest, only 3 ins. high, are the gems that will
stand the frost and poke their noses through the snow.

The chequered lily, the Snake's-Head Fritillary, with superb
pendant flowers of lilac, dark purple and white, many of them
meticulously spotted, has a fascination of its own and flowers in
April or May. (The 'Crown Imperial', *F. Imperialis*, is a member of
this family. Yellow, orange and bronze hanging bells, crested with
a crown of glossy, green foliage. March-April. $2\frac{1}{2}$ ft.)

So much for the spring bulbs, and on to the Autumn Crocus and
Colchicums. Misty lavender Autumn Crocus speciosus with its
vivid golden anthers and orange stigma, gives colour when there is
little about, and the Colchicum or Meadow Saffron is also welcome
in October, even if its bold eighteen-inch foliage becomes cumber-
some in the spring. 'Lilac Wonder', with a tinge of pink and thin
white stripe on each petal, is a beautiful hybrid and, happily sited,
has proved itself a robust Londoner.

Some of the Summer-flowering Bulbs and Bulbous Plants

The ornamental garlics, the Alliums, are steadily growing more
popular. They are interesting hardy bulbous plants, many of them
willing to grow anywhere and likely to survive their owner.

Their flat umbels and round heads solidly tasselled that delight
the flower arranger, are unique and striking. The Alliums enjoy a
sunny position and a sandy loam soil and should be planted 3 ins.
deep. Deadheading is important, otherwise the garden may be
overrun with seedlings.

A. albopilosum has large lilac heads. 12-18 ins. *A. moly* is an old favourite with broad glaucous leaves and bright yellow umbels. 12 ins. *A. azureum* has globular heads of sky-blue. 1-2 ft.

There are also a number of handsome pink and crimson varieties.

The *Amaryllis belladonna* is for gardeners in the south who have warm soil and perhaps a south wall to offer. The pink trumpets that arrive before the foliage are magnificent. June or July are the best months for planting—4 ins. deep. Winter protection of spent hops or bracken should be given.

Sun-loving *Galtonia candicans* is a 4-ft. summer-flowering, dignified-looking snowdrop, sometimes known as *Hyacinthus candicans*. February to April are the best months for planting 6 ins. deep, and later on staking is a wise precaution.

Gladiolus

There is a long list of the grand large-flowered varieties, the waved and fluffy-petalled butterflies, the shorter and slender-stemmed primulinus with their florets loosely set, and the even smaller mignon group.

They are sun-lovers, requiring a moisture-retaining soil well dug and enriched with humus.

Early March is a good time for planting but the ground should be reasonably dry and free from frost. Corms should be planted 4-6 ins. deep according to size, and are better placed in a trench than put in by dibber, allowing at least 6-7 ins. between each corm. A sprinkling of coarse sand beneath and above the corm is beneficial and assists lifting later on.

If there is a dry spell after the corms have started into growth, they must not be allowed to go dry.

The plant is sometimes attacked by a small black insect, the thrips, in which case, it must be sprayed regularly with Sybol or DDT.

If cutting the flower spikes, at least four leaves must be left on the stem, otherwise, the corms will suffer.

About six weeks after flowering, and before the foliage has turned yellow, the corms should be lifted, cutting off the stems to an inch or so above the corm and dusting with DDT powder. They should then be spread out in a greenhouse or sunny place for three or four weeks before cleaning off the outer husk and dusting once more with DDT.

Finally, the corms should be stored in an airy, dry, frost-proof place in an open container.

Medium high-crowned corms often give as good spikes as the large fat ones. They should, whenever possible, be planted on a different site every year.

When it comes to varieties, some of the best types will be found among the reds and pinks and fancy-frilled novelties, while lemon-green 'Woodpecker' with wine-red markings is as yet the most beautiful of them all.

Cross-breeding with the superb scented Acidanthera goes forward and breeders are hopeful of arriving at a sweet-scented Gladiolus. But scent is often evasive.

Lilies

This is a diverse family and it is impossible to generalize on the Lily's likes and dislikes other than that they all demand a well-drained soil and benefit by sitting on a cushion of coarse sand.

Some will tolerate a little lime, others shrink from it: some bulb breeders advocate a generous humus content in the soil, but there are those that believe it is dangerous, spreading disease.

Leaf-mould is the lily's favourite diet, but it is the general opinion that it is safe to mulch with well-rotted manure.

The gardener should, whenever possible, inspect the bulbs before buying, to make sure that they are healthy, with basal roots intact. The earlier in the autumn they can be bought, the better, so that they can settle in before the frost. The Lilies should be planted immediately on arrival as the fleshy-scaled bulb soon dehydrates; their new home should be ready waiting for them.

With the exception of the Madonna Lily that enjoys the sun and open border, the Lilies prefer partial shade and their heads in the sun in the same way as the Clematis.

Depth of planting will depend on the type of the Lily. If stem-rooting (producing roots from the stem above the bulb), it will require planting about 6 ins. deep, adding a mulch of some 3 ins. to the surface soil.

Those sending out roots from the base of the bulb should, if large, be planted 4-6 ins. deep, but in the case of the small, only 3-4 ins. deep.

The townsman should grow the more stalwart species that have proved themselves easy-going.

Stem-rooting *Lilium regale* from Western China must head the list, being the easiest of them all. After only sixty years' cultivation in this country, its white funnel-shaped trumpets streaked with brown outside and shaded with gold within are seen in gardens big and small throughout July. *L. regale album*, the pure white form, has lovely substance.

L. martagon (Turk's Cap) in various forms, with light purple pendulous flowers spotted with varying shades of purple, the fleshy blooms with recurving segments, presents no difficulties.

Deep orange spotted brown *L. henryi* is exceedingly hardy and vigorous and I have seen it reach to 7 ft. in a chimney-pot area, while *L. willmottiae*'s reflexed orange flowers are often seen in built-up areas.

L. speciosum and *tigrinum*, the Tiger Lily, and perhaps *L. pardalinum*, the Californian Lily, if you have a shady, rather damp corner to offer, should be given a trial.

The modern Bellingham and Mid-Century Hybrids are easy, vigorous and comparatively cheap. Erect orange 'Enchantment' is one of the most successful of these.

Now I come to the more temperamental. *L. auratum*, the Golden Ray Lily of Japan, the pure white beauty decorated with crimson and brown spots and golden bands, is a glory. But alas, I have so often seen it disappear without rhyme or reason just when it appeared to have settled down that I have lost faith in its reliability. But it is such a wonder that some gardeners will think it worth growing if for a single performance only.

The Madonna Lily, *L. candidum*, can be moody too. She should not be deep planted, and covered with no more than 1 in. of light soil. She will be seen to do well in strangely diverse conditions, but undoubtedly misses country life and the cottage garden.

Montbretia

The neglected orange Montbretia and the washy-blue Lupin have haunted neglected gardens decade upon decade. But the modern

Montbretia, more properly known as *Crocosmia × crocosmiaeflora*, is a delightful bulbous plant with flowers of greater size than before in a new colour range from clear yellow through pink to crimson.

Unfortunately they are not as hardy as their tough orange predecessor, and in cold areas, like Gladioli, they are better lifted and planted out the following April. They should be found a well-drained place and planted 3 ins. deep.

Tigridia

The Eastern-looking Tiger Flower should only be planted by the townsman in the south or west and must be given a well-drained position and a light warm soil.

T. pavonia, growing to 1-2 ft., has exotic flowers in bright red and yellow shades with striking markings. They last but a day, but there is a succession of bloom ready to take over throughout August. This exciting bulbous-rooted plant should be planted in April, lifted in October, and planted 3 ins. deep. It is a star turn.

21 Herbs

The vogue for cultivating herbs seems to have died down from the middle of the seventeenth century: no doubt the popularity of the flower garden in the eighteenth century had something to do with the eclipse of the herbals.

Now that we are more interested in food and flavour they are back in favour. Cartwheels with parsley, chives and thyme planted between the spikes and ladders with mint growing between the rungs are quite a common sight. Small enclosures in the form of a knot garden patterned with box are effective but difficult to keep going in grimy conditions.

Herbs are inclined to be woody and untidy. What they need is the sun and a position sheltered against the prevailing winds, somewhere near the kitchen door. After all, this is the cook's garden; whether large or small, it should be utilitarian.

Cultivation and Harvesting

Most of the herbs are easy-going and are content with a good ordinary soil well aerated. They should be watered during a dry summer and some of the perennials lifted and divided every three years.

Town gardeners in difficult areas should plant in the spring. Regular hoeing and a light peat mulch will help to conserve moisture and keep down the competitive weeds.

Herbs gathered for drying should be picked before they come into flower when their flavour is pronounced. There are exceptions to this rule, among them tarragon, which is best picked in August.

Shoots should be picked in the morning before the hot midday sun is on the plants, but they must be dry. Plants should not be severely robbed at one picking but small bunches taken at different times.

The delicate fragrance of the Bouquet Garni is most rewarding, and the famous cook, Mrs Isabella Beeton, describes the little bunch as consisting of two or three sprigs of parsley, a sprig of thyme and a bay leaf, with the addition of marjoram, celery leaves and basil.

There are a number of books on the growing and harvesting of herbs so I name only those likely to be in constant use by the not too demanding cook.

A List of Useful Herbs

Balm. A hardy perennial. Stems should be gathered when the flowers open, and dried. Balm tea, sometimes used with Indian tea, is a lemon-flavoured infusion. Propagation by division in October-March.

Basil. Sweet basil, much in favour in France for fish, soups and sauces, is difficult to grow in this country. The bush basil is a hardier plant but should be raised under glass and planted out at the end of May.

Bergamot, the monarda, is a handsome perennial. The leaves may be used in salads, or mixed with cress as a salad dressing. Propagation by division in spring or autumn.

Borage. A hardy annual. The leaves are excellent for flavouring claret cups and Pimms No. 1. Seed can be sown in autumn or spring.

Chervil. An annual with cut leaves used for flavouring soups, fish, stews and salads. Seeds may be sown outdoors in March or under glass in October.

Chives. A bulbous-rooted hardy perennial and a good neat town grower more delicate in taste than the onion. Delicious for egg dishes, cream cheese flavouring and salads. At the moment in danger of being rather indiscriminately used. Propagation by division every three years.

Cutting with scissors spares the chive, parsley and other herbs in constant use, wear and tear.

Dandelion, so popular in Elizabethan times, is seldom used these days. Propagation by seed sown in the spring.

Fennel. A hardy perennial with delightful fern-like foliage, growing to 2-3 ft. Excellent flavouring for fish, salads and sauces. Deadheading is advised. Propagation by seed sown in April.

Horseradish. A possessive rampant grower that must be firmly controlled, otherwise it will take command. Horseradish is not only good with roast beef, but even better with white fish. The Swedes make a delectable apple sauce with white wine and a taste of horseradish.

Marjoram. A perennial, often a chef's favourite for flavouring soups. Propagation by division in the autumn.

Mint. Some seedsmen supply five or more different varieties of mints; the large-leaved are recommended for cooking with peas, but the round-leaved *Mentha rotundifolia*, the apple mint, has a subtler flavour. Spearmint is usually the basis for mint sauce. The mint bed should be watered freedly during the summer, the stems cut down in September, and the plants top-dressed with compost. Propagation by division in the autumn or spring cuttings.

Parsley. A hardy perennial, and an indispensable pot-herb for the kitchen. It is not always as well grown as it should be, its liking for lime being overlooked. Sensitive as it is to damp and heavy air pollution in towns, seed should be sown from February to late summer for succession and against casualties. Foliage that coarsens should be cut back to induce fresh young growth.

Rue is too biting and pungent for most of us and should perhaps be confined to the flower border, where its glaucous foliage is welcome. 'Jackman's Blue' is particularly pleasing.

Sage. A hardy perennial used for flavouring game and sausagemeat. The broad-leaf, non-flowering sage is the best culinary variety. Plants are best kept young and spring cuttings taken every year.

Sorrel. The large-leaved perennial French Oseille de Belville is recommended for soups, being less bitter than the English varieties. Propagation by division in the spring, or by seed in March.

Tarragon. A good-looking and useful herb requiring plenty of space, and again the French variety is recommended for use in salads and egg dishes. Sprigs steeped in wine-vinegar can be set aside for winter use. Propagation by division in spring, or by August or September cuttings (with a heel to them when possible).

Thyme. A hardy perennial without which a Bouquet Garni is incomplete. Young shoots gathered during the flowering season should be dried for the winter. Propagation is by division and cuttings in the spring.

The erudite cook will make useful additions to this list and the gardener, when planning, must see to it that there is a bay tree near the kitchen door.

22 *The Rock Garden*

If rocks are to be introduced and flowers grown among them, the size, height of the mountains, peaks and slopes must be carefully designed and in proportion with the garden as a whole. There are far too many outcrops and unplanned eruptions about that have no right to call themselves rockeries.

Only rarely has the town garden the perfect rock garden site to offer, with the required slope and the desired fall to the south or at least south-west. Trees must be avoided, for the best of the rockery plants and treasured alpines crave for the sun and die if exposed to the drip from overhanging branches and the fall of dank leaves.

The choice of stone is decided by the size of the budget, but sandstone and limestone are two of the best-looking. A visit to the stone merchant is advised in order to pick out rocks with a happy striation of graining.

One-third of the rock must be embedded in the soil and the strata placed so that it runs one way as in nature.

The spongy yellow-brown tufa rock available from the alpine nurseryman is loved by lime-tolerant alpines and unfortunately by pigeons too. Some gardeners net the tufa once it is planted up in defence of plants and rock.

Although tufa is more difficult to place than sandstone or limestone, it has the advantage of absorbing and holding moisture and provides the plants with a pleasant cool root run. It is unlikely to be everlasting, but disintegrates slowly.

Concrete and other artificial materials that masquerade as rocks are seldom sympathetic or satisfying.

Drainage must be immaculate so that the rain has a ready outlet. Much will depend on the lie of the land but it may be necessary to dig a ditch or provide a soakaway.

Once the stage is set, the site must be intensively weeded so that every perennial weed is meticulously removed, root and all. A selective weedkiller is a time-saver or sodium chlorate may be used if the gardener is prepared to leave the site unplanted for six months.

Soil

Most rock plants and alpines are content in a fairly acid soil. A good loam, plus a generous addition of leaf-mould or peat, grit and coarse sand will satisfy most of them. The grit should be coarse and the peat, horticultural or otherwise, moist.

Once the plants are accommodated individually in their own small pockets, it is easy to give the lime-lovers special treatment and their beloved limestone chips.

Hoof and horn may be worked into the soil from time to time, but quick-acting pep fertilizers should not be used in the rock garden.

The Alpine Meadow or Lawn

There is no reason why all but the delicate and sensitive rock plants and alpines should not be grown in the open, without rocks. They are often seen growing this way in Austria and Switzerland, where in spring great expanses, sloped and flat, are carpeted with creeping ground-huggers.

I am not suggesting that the townsman is in possession of meadows and far-stretching slopes, but a number have a small patch of unsatisfactory and rather meaningless lawn that might well be better dug up and planted with rockery plants. Many gardeners would no doubt be pleased to put the mower away.

Once again the drainage must be satisfactory and the ground well prepared with an addition of sand and grit.

The cool root run provided by the stones is not an essential to such plants as the white, pink and crimson Thrift, or the many different coloured species and varieties of Thymes. Here is a place where the Acaena and other rampers will be welcome. *A. buchananii*, with its white-grey foliage and yellow burr-headed flowers, and bronze-green foliaged crimson-flowering *A. micro-*

phylla will cover the naked ground like a flood, given the sun and a congenial diet.

Aubrietias, Campanulas and Dianthus will willingly join in this tapestry work, and there is always the Chamomile, used so freely in the seventeenth century as a lawn, to fill in difficult places.

Meanwhile, the lawn will suit an army of spring bulbs, the Crocuses can be followed by drifts of *Narcissus asturiensis* (syn. *minimus*), metallic-blue *Scilla siberica* and yellow and purple-blue dwarf Irises. Four-inch cream-yellow May-flowering *Tulipa batalinii* or golden-yellow *T. tarda*, white-tipped inside with purple markings outside, only 3 ins. high, are always ready to follow on after the Narcissus. And finally, when the trees turn to colour, the autumn-flowering Crocus will ring down the curtain.

It is hoped that the lists that follow will be found helpful, but I feel I should point out that for the town garden in very unpromising surroundings suffering air-pollution, only the toughest subjects will survive. Among them are:

Alyssum saxatile	Heuchera
Arabis	Oxalis
Aubrietia	Saxifraga
Campanula cochlearifolia	Stonecrops (and in particular
Centranthus	the Houseleek)
Cerastium	Veronica

Alpine List for Towns With Favourable Conditions to Offer

Spring

Adonis amurensis plena. Yellow. 9-12 ins.
Aethionema coridifolium 'Warley Rose'. Rose-pink. 4-6 ins.
Aquilegia alpina. Bright blue. 8 ins.
Campanula arvatica. Large violet stars. 2 ins.
C. garganica 'W. H. Payne'. Dark blue with white eye. 4 ins.
Cyananthus lobatus. White. 4 ins.
Epimedium, various. 4-9 ins.
Gentiana acaulis. Deep blue trumpets. 3-4 ins.
G. verna. Vivid blue, cross-shaped flowers. Difficult. 2 ins.
Phlox douglasii 'May Snow'. 2 ins.
P. d. 'Boothman's Variety'. Mauve with violet centre. 2 ins.
P. d. 'Rosea'. Silvery-pink. 2 ins.

White Christening rose 'Bianca' in a garden in Genoa

A paved courtyard designed by A. du Gard Pasley. Plants include
Mahonia japonica, the variegated Ivy, *Hedera Helix* 'Gloire de Marengo',
recumbent Junipers and lace-cap Hydrangeas

P. subulata (Mossy Phlox) 'Sprite'. Pink with carmine eye. 4 ins.
P. s. 'Temiscaming'. Deep red. 4 ins.
Pulsatilla vulgaris (Pasque Flower). Purple-violet, golden stamens, silky stems. 12 ins.

Summer

Achillea rupestris. Pure white. 6 ins.
A. × *tomentosa* (*lewisii*) King Edward. Sulphur-yellow. 6 ins.
Campanula Birch Hybrid. Violet. 6 ins.
Ceratostigma plumbaginoides. Reddish stems, blue flowers. 12-15 ins.
Dianthus deltoides 'Brilliant'. Magenta-crimson. 6 ins.
Dryas sundermannii. Pure white, golden stamens. 4-6 ins.
Fuchsia 'Tom Thumb'. Rose and purple. 9 ins.
Globularia 'Globe Daisy'. Blue. 3 ins.
Gypsophila 'Rosy Veil'. Double pink. 12 ins.
Iberis sempervirens 'Little Gem'. White. 6 ins.
Lewisia howellii. Apricot-striped rose. 6 ins.
Potentilla aurea plena. Yellow. 2 ins.
P. fragiformis. Bright yellow. 9 ins.
P. nepalensis 'Miss Willmott'. Cherry-red. 6-12 ins.
Miniature Roses:
    'Humpty Dumpty'. Rich pink.
    'Baby Masquerade'. Multicoloured.
    'Tinker Bell'. Pink.
    'Yellow Doll'. Pure yellow.
Saxifraga primuloides 'Elliott's Variety'. (Small edition of London Pride). 8 ins.
Sedum cauticola. Rose-purple. 3 ins.
S. telephium × *spectabile* 'Autumn Joy'. Red-purple. 12 ins.
Statice (syn. *Limonium*) *bellidifolium.* Pale lilac. 6-9 ins.

Winter

Spring Bulbs

Winter-flowering Crocus species
Cyclamen neapolitanum
Galanthus, various

Iris danfordiae
I. histrioides
I. reticulata

Shrubs

Clematis balearica   Mahonia, new dwarf forms
Erica carnea, various. 6-9 ins.

Sinks and Trough Gardens

Miniature rock gardens have a fascination and certain alpines benefit by the extra care they get in a garden of such manageable size.

The desirable container has become difficult to buy. Whatever
the shape or size, it is all-important that it should have drainage
holes. If absent, they should be cut with a stonemason's imple-
ment.

The sink should be given an open position facing west where it
gets the sun. It may be placed on a pedestal and looks particularly
well on a low wall, but in any case it should be raised from the
ground out of the way of dogs, cats and all but the energetic snail
or slug.

Soil and special cosseting of the lime-haters is the same for the
miniature estate as for the normal rockery.

Here is the opportunity for a gardener interested in a particular
genus such as the Gentian that does not readily mix with others,
or perhaps the delightful Alpine Pinks.

The town gardener would be wise to plant such treasures in the
spring rather than in the autumn.

Trough Collection

Antennaria dioica rosea   *Micromeria corsica*
Asperula lilaciflora   *Mentha requienii*
Campanula pilosa major   *Potentilla aurea plena*
Dianthus 'Grenadier'   *Rosa roulettii*
Erinus 'Dr Haenaele'   *Saponaria caespitosa*
Gentiana farreri   *Saxifraga lingulata*
Iris lacustris   *S. oppositifolia splendens*
Lewisia howellii   *Sempervivum arachnoideum*

33 Ground Cover

Upkeep is sometimes a problem even in a small town garden. There may be a lack of time or money, or for physical reasons the owner of the garden may be unfit to ply the hoe, much less dig.

The modern answer to this problem is ground-cover plants that will reduce the need for digging and weeding, and among them are shrubs, roses, herbaceous plants, perennials and annuals, foliage plants—rampers, smotherers, trailers, carpeters and ground-huggers.

All these should be strong and willing maids of all work.

First they should be vigorous enough not only to compete with the weeds, but to win the battle for existence. Half-hearted and easily discouraged growers are useless as suppressors and the weeds seem to enjoy downing them.

The tough, short, spreading subjects that will look after themselves, tolerate poorish soil and partial shade, and carpet a bare patch of naked earth in a reasonable time are the plants to look for.

It is important to set the ground coverers off to a good start in a rich and suitable soil so that they will not need further attention, other than thinning to prevent the more vigorous ousting their neighbours.

It is vital that all perennial weeds should be removed at the start, for it is extremely difficult to get rid of them once the carpet has formed.

Watering may be necessary in the early stages after planting, but once the plants begin to fulfil their function they will, by covering the soil, conserve the moisture.

Shrubs

Low-growing, prostrate and creeping shrubs are helpful in reducing weeding and upkeep.

Much will depend on the gardener's soil, but the catalogues available from the nurseryman give a wide choice and offer special
small ground-cover collections.

Many of the **Cotoneasters** will serve the purpose. *C. dammeri*
has the advantage of being evergreen, but *C. horizontalis*'s fan-
shaped branches defeat the weeds equally well.

The flat growing **Cytisus procumbens** will cover five or six
square feet of ground and has cheerful bright yellow flowers.
C. × *kewensis* is prostrate with profuse cream flowers.

If you happen to be on lime-free soil, there is the large Heath
family to choose from, but it should be remembered that **Erica
carnea** is one of the few members of the family prepared to face a
taste of lime.

Euonymus radicans variegatus makes a dense evergreen
carpet, the small foliage edged with white becomes pink-tinted in
winter.

Fatshedera × lizei, the grand bigeneric hybrid between the
Irish Ivy and the Japanese Fatsia, is an extremely handsome plant.
Its green shiny foliage is most effective in covering an awkward
corner or bank shirked by the mower.

Many of the **Genistas** are robust creepers and golden-yellow-
flowering *G. lydia* is an outstanding dwarf shrub.

When it comes to the **Hederas** or Ivies, the choice is tremendous,
and the Ivy is a splendid covering for bare ground under trees
where grass will not grow. A planting of green and variegated
gold and silver varieties, cleverly patterned, can be made a decorative feature.

H. helix 'Buttercup' is the best golden ivy; *H. chicago variegata*,
often grown as a house plant, will often settle in the garden; *H.
cristata* has crinkly-edged leaves; *H. canariensis*, with golden
variegated foliage, sometimes temperamental, is worth trying;
H. marginata 'Silver Queen' should also be given a chance, along
with *H. discolor* (syn. *marmorata*) 'Minor'. *H. glacier*, with small
white-edged leaves is trailing; *H. luzi* is a delightful slow-growing

miniature that is good company for little German yellow-centred 'Jubilee'.

Hypericum or 'St John's Wort' has, during the last decade, done noble service in covering unwanted land, and the rampant *H. calycinum* planting has become monotonous. However, the large *H. patulum* 'Hidcote' with its fine yellow flowers is a chalk-lover that should not be overlooked.

The creeping mat-forming **Junipers** are ideal for limy soils and *horizontalis* will cover large areas with its blue leaves.

Mahonia japonica is a first-rate shrub with winter clusters of long pendulous lemon-yellow racemes that are as fragrant as the lily of the valley. *M. aquifolium* is cheaper, but not so glamorous.

The shrubby **Polygala** with pea-shaped flowers and the dwarf Milkwort, only an inch or two high, deserve consideration if the soil is lime-free.

The **Potentilla** dwarfs that thrive in any soil make delightful colonies and, when happy, flower profusely.

Gardeners on peat will have the advantage of being able to grow the low-growing and dwarf evergreen **Rhododendron**. 'Bluebird' and 'Blue Diamond' are excellent hybrids, while 'Blue Tit' will form dense bushes covering $2\frac{1}{2}$ ft.

The **Skimmia** with bright-red winter berries seems to like town life but it is slow in covering the ground.

The **Vinca** or Periwinkle, with white, blue or purple flowers, is fast-growing and invasive and must be regularly checked, otherwise it will take over.

Ground-cover Plants

Every gardener has his own favourite selection of weed smotherers and here are some of mine.

Acaena microphylla. Bronze foliage, red flowered bracts; a good carpeter. 2 ins.

Ajuga reptans brockbankii, the blue bugle. 6 ins.

Alchemilla mollis (Lady's Mantle), with sulphur-green flowers. 9 ins.

Bergenia cordifolia (Elephant's Ears). Pink, apple-blossom or magenta, a superb evergreen ground cover plant. Ballawley Hybrid with green leaves that turn to red and mahogany in winter and the new German hybrids are outstanding. A splendid plant that looks after itself. 12 ins.

Campanula poscharskyana, with masses of bright green foliage and profuse light blue summer flowers. 9 ins.

Cornus canadensis, the perfect carpeter, with flat rosette leaves and white-bracted spring flowers of singular charm. This is a deciduous creeper, the foliage developing rich autumn tints before it falls. 6 ins.

Dryas octopetala if on lime-free soil. A carpeter with large white flowers in spring. 3 ins.

Epimediums, yellow spring flowerers, yellow, crimson and white, capable of defeating all competitors with their powerful roots. 6-12 ins.

Geraniums. The Cranesbill makes an excellent ground-cover plant for shady positions. *G. endressii* with silver pink flowers and 'Johnson's Blue' are two of the best. 9-12 ins.

The **Hostas** (syn. Funkia) are a wonderfully diverse and trouble-free family. They make luxuriant spring and summer growth, but, being deciduous, their large, glaucous, dark and light-green variegated and differently margined leaves die away in late autumn. *Hosta lancifolia* has green leaves and lilac flowers. *H. l. albo marginata* white-edged narrow leaves, and *H. l. aurea* foliage tinged gold.

H. sieboldiana has glaucous heart-shaped leaves, and *H. undulata medio variegata* has creamy-white variegations. These are but a few of the many attractive members of this family.

Lamium maculatum aureum has delightful variegated foliage, is easier to control than some of its persistent relations, and has mauve winter flowers. 12 ins.

Prunella forms a neat carpet if the stubby flower spikes are cut back after flowering. *P. grandiflora incisa* has purple flowers from June until October. 9 ins.

The grey woolly leaves of **Stachys lanata** are delightful, but to succeed the little plant requires a clean, sunny atmosphere. 18 ins.

The **Alpine Strawberry** will cover the ground and supply delicious fruit from May until the late autumn for those who have the patience to pick it. But it can become a trespasser. 3 ins.

Tiarella cordifolia, the Foam Flower, with fluffy cream flowers, enjoys a moist partially-shaded position. 9 ins.

Warning

I would warn gardeners that ground-cover plants, because they are and have to be persistent and determined, need a firm hand, otherwise they will take control. I once inherited a garden where *Cerastium tomentosum*, white flowering 'Snow-in-Summer', had had the free run of the garden for a decade. I never managed to master the plant, much less get rid of it.

24 The Shaded Garden

The number of plants found willing to grow in towns even in the shade is increasing rapidly.

The failure of many in the past was falsely put down to atmospheric pollution or lack of sun and air. It has since been discovered that the majority of demises were due to the hungry and lifeless soil, the acidic deposit of years having defeated all bacteria so essential to plant life.

Complete replacement or drastic renovation of the soil is the only remedy for this sad condition. Humus, manure or compost must be generously introduced.

Few town gardeners have room for a compost heap of any size, and farmyard manure becomes scarcer every day. However, humus in any form, peat, hop-manure, organics such as hoof and horn, and dried blood as a quick pick-me-up will all serve as the required nutriment.

Meanwhile, the hoe should be kept moving so that the hard soil crust so often seen beneath trees has not the time to form and the soil is kept healthy and aerated.

In some cases, a lime dressing before feeding is beneficial, but not of course in gardens where there are Rhododendrons, Azaleas and ericaceous subjects.

There are degrees of shade, from the lightly dappled to the almost complete darkness of borders and beds overhung by giant trees, so that the suggestions I give will not apply to gardens one and all.

In deep shade where the garden is overhung with deciduous trees the early spring bulbs and flowerers that give their performance before the trees are in full leaf should play an important part.

Meanwhile, the dark garden is no longer the calamity that it was—with spotlighting, an interesting statue or perhaps a fountain and carefully chosen greenery it can be surprisingly beautiful, or, better still, mysterious.

The list at the end of this chapter is by no means exhaustive and gardeners will wish to add to it and make their own experiments. It is a game of hit and miss, often with pleasant surprises.

I have tried out most of the shrubs and plants mentioned in a garden in Holland Park, London, that was my home for six years; the remainder have been grown with success by my friends in other parts of London.

Here are some of the shrubs and plants most likely to succeed in the shade. Rhododendrons, Azaleas, and others insist on a lime-free soil.

Shrubs

Aucuba japonica
Azalea
Bamboos
Berberis × *stenophylla*
Camellia
Deutzia
Euonymus japonica
Fatsia japonica
Fuchsia magellanica vars.
Holly (including the variegated forms)
Hydrangea
Hypericum
Kerria japonica plena

Laurustinus
Ligustrum ovalifolium (Oval-leaf-Privet) and *L. aureo marginatum* (Golden Privet). This will light up a dark corner.
Mahonia japonica
Mock Orange
Osmanthus
Pieris
Rhododendron
Skimmia
Snowberry
Syringa (Lilac)

Climbers

Ampelopsis (*Vitis inconstans*)
Chaenomeles (Japanese Quince). Not technically a climber, but easily trained.
Cotoneaster horizontalis
Fatshedera × *lizei*. A cross between Ivy and Fatsia—an excellent subject for shade, but requires training.

Jasminum nudiflorum (Winter Jasmine)
Pyracantha (Firethorn)

Perennials

Anemone japonica (Japanese Anemone)
Asperula odorata (Woodruff)
Campanula. *Glomerata* is among the tolerant. Deep-blue *C. latiloba* is a splendid plant.
Dicentra eximea (Bleeding Heart)
Digitalis (Foxglove)
Doronicum (Leopard's Bane)
Euphorbia (Spurge). There are a host of Euphorbias that manage in partial shade. *E. robbiae* is particularly useful, with long-lasting bright green flowers. *E. dulcis* is best known for its autumn colour, while *E. wulfenii*, a semi-shrub with yellow flowers, may well be the most adaptable.
Ferns. Various, including the Hartstongue, the Shield Fern, both possessing fascinating fronds, and the Royal Fern, *Osmunda regalis*. This is the largest and noblest of our native species. When content, in damp favoured places, the fibrous-rooted clump sends up fronds to a height of 5 or 6 ft. The Royal Fern is sometimes known as the Flowering Fern, the spore-bearing region of the frond being carried high, giving the appearance of small brown flowers.
   Geraniums. Various. Violet *G. pratense plenum* and salmon-pink *G. endressii* 'Wargrave' are recommended.
   Hemerocallis (Day Lily). There is a large choice of interesting new American varieties.
   Heucherella. This interesting introduction with pink spires should be tried both in sun and partial shade.
   Hosta. Various. Preferably not variegated for shade.
Iberis sempervirens (Candytuft)
Iris germanica.
Lobelia fulgens. *L. f.* 'Bee's Flame', intense, scarlet—temperamental but worth trying.
   Monarda (Bergamot). Red, pink and mauve. Enjoys moist shade.
   Phlox paniculata (decussata). The white perennial phlox does well in light shade.

Polygonatum (Solomon's Seal), a great standby.

Primula (Primrose) *polyanthus*, including the new blue and pink strains. *P. denticulata* (Drumstick).

Thalictrum (Meadow Rue). Various, tolerant of partial shade.

Tradescantia (Moses-in-the-Bulrushes).

Trillium. A woodland lover. White and pink, spring.

Viola. *V. cornuta*, white, purple and mauve, will grow in partial shade.

Annuals

Annuals are, as a rule, too much in a hurry to rest and enjoy the shade. However, here are a few that will adapt themselves.

Humulus (Hop). Also the golden form.

Lavatera (Mallow). 'Loveliness' is a charming rose-pink.

Linum (Flax).

Lunaria (Honesty). White and purple, silver seed-pods.

Malcolmia (Stock). Single varieties should be tried.

Nigella damascena (Love-in-a-Mist).

Rheum palmatum. An attractive ornamental rhubarb with brown-red leaves.

Tropaeolum (Nasturtium). *T. peregrinum* (Canary Creeper).

Grasses

Ornamental grasses, increasing in popularity, will succeed in partial shade. *Microlaena stipoides* is useful and withstands drought under trees.

Bulbs

Most bulbs will give a single performance after planting as they have their own store-room. The following bulbs or corms will, if left in the ground undisturbed, naturalize themselves and increase.

Aconite (Eranthis or Winter Aconite).

Anemone. *A. blanda*, the wild Windflower, and others.

Blue bell.

Colchicum. Autumn-flowering, pink and mauve, and the rare yellow form with large fleshy foliage in spring.

Convallaria (Lily of the Valley).

Cyclamen. Hardy. Will grow happily among tree roots in cool shady conditions.

Erythronium (Dog's-Tooth Violet). White, pink and lavender.

Fritillary. *F. meleagris*, small, chequered white, mauve and purple. *F. imperialis*, Crown Imperial, stately—yellow and orange, green leaves, crown pendulous flowers.

Galanthus (Snowdrop). Favours partial shade.

Leucojum (Snowflake). Spring and autumn.

Lilium, various.

Muscari (Grape Hyacinth). Blue and white.

Ornithogalum. *O. umbellatum* (Star of Bethlehem). *O. nutans*, grey and silver and unusual.

Scilla. *S. siberica*, blue, pink and white. *S. campanulata*.

Note: Crocus like to bask in the sun and give an inferior display in the shade. Narcissi give a good performance their first year, but if the shade is considerable, are likely to deteriorate and finally disappear. The tuberous Begonia does well in the shade but must be lifted before there is any danger of frost.

Ground Cover

The chapter on this subject should be consulted, but the following subjects will be found particularly co-operative as ground cover.

Galeobdalon aureum can compete with full shade.

Hedera (Ivy)

Hypericum (Rose of Sharon)

Lamium (Dead-Nettle)

Pteris aquilina (Bracken). Difficult.

Vinca (Periwinkle).

25 Window-Boxes

Window-box gardening has always fascinated me. The fact that my book on the subject has sold some 50,000 copies in hard back and paperback and is still in demand goes to show the tremendous interest there is in the subject.

A gay box of window-sill flowers will cheer up the gloomiest of streets, and be a solace to the gardener who for some reason or other may be confined to the house.

Window-box gardening is a rewarding pursuit, a form of social welfare within the reach of almost anyone. All that is needed is a container and eight or so inches of soil, plus a sixpenny packet of 'Cherry Rose' or mixed Nasturtiums. Or should the street be sunless, a few Begonia tubers and six rosettes of London Pride or perhaps a handful of cuttings of the Victorian *Campanula isophylla* wheedled from a grandmother.

The Box

There are window-boxes for all tastes and purses, from Florentine pottery to British plastic. They can, of course, be home-made in teak, oak, ash, elm or deal, to last a year or two or a decade.

Wooden boxes should be treated with a preservative such as Cuprinol, (S.Q.D.) brushing the liquid well into the joints. Creosote, poisonous to plants, should not be used.

Whatever the material, the boxes must have adequate drainage holes and be wide and deep enough to accommodate Geraniums and other plants when turned out of pots without disturbing their root-ball. A 3 ft. long box, 9 ins. deep and 10 ins. wide, will be found a useful all-purpose size.

The deal box will require several coats of lead paint followed by two coats of ordinary paint if it is to last. A town box, to be kept smart, will need re-painting every other year.

Lastly, for the safety of pedestrians below, it is the duty of the gardener to see that his window-box is secure. If he wishes to keep in favour with his landlord it will be worth his while to provide his window-boxes with drip-trays.

Soil

Town soil is not always easy to come by, but I have dealt with this subject in a previous chapter (see p. 13). A good peat content is a life-saver; it holds the moisture and prevents clogging.

John Innes No. 3 Compost, a carefully balanced mixture available from a nursery, sundriesman or garden centre, serves the purpose well. Ordinary garden soil is seldom good enough; if used, 4 ozs. of bonemeal or superphosphate and a double handful of peat should be added to each box and well mixed in.

Where there is heavy air pollution, it may be necessary to change the soil every year. The window-box owner must beware of being over-economical or even a little mean in carrying out this important operation until he learns the facts of life: that plants will not grow strongly unless well fed.

Before introducing the soil, the box must be carefully and generously crocked so that fast and effective drainage is ensured. The crocks should be covered with roughage (the coarser part of the compost, the residue of sieving) to prevent clogging.

The Plantings

Window-box gardening often turns out more expensive than the owner has anticipated, particularly if a non-stop show is expected the whole year through.

I used to enjoy helping a rich and extravagant owner plan five plantings. Top-sized bulbs of Tulip specie and distinguished Daffodils were country-grown in pots ready for dropping into the box in March. These were followed by blue Polyanthus and Forget-me-nots that held the fort until the Geraniums were ready. These came from a Geranium specialist and the reds, pinks and whites made a glorious splash. One summer, when the bad sunless

174

weather defeated them, they were replaced by a short-lived box of blue conservatory-grown Cinerarias. Chrysanthemums followed, and stayed only a short time before being replaced by a winter planting of dwarf, interesting and colourful small shrubs, berried or variegated, thickly interplanted with blue, golden-crested *Iris histrioides major*, which poked their noses through the snow in January.

This extravagant way of planting is showmanship rather than gardening. Flowers opened and faded and were quickly swept away, but the pleasure of seeing plants grow is missed.

Three plantings should satisfy the demanding, while two plantings will meet the wishes of most of us. They are the autumn planting of bulbs, among them Daffodils, Tulips, Crocus and Scillas, and the summer planting that will remain until the frost.

Zonal and Ivy-leaved Geraniums are undoubtedly the best window-box plants we possess, provided they get plenty of sun. If the box is in the shade, then the blue riband must go to the tuberous Begonia.

Geraniums should be bought from a specialist in order not only to escape from 'Paul Crampel' and 'Gustave Emich', but to get to know the less startling American Irene varieties, pastel beauties and the endearing miniatures.

I think the mixed geranium box interplanted perhaps with the variegated-foliaged Victorian 'L'Elegante' is the most beautiful of all. The clash of colour is pleasant rather than upsetting. The ivy-leaved that will hang over the edge of the box should be more generously planted than the rest, and in particular lovely double imperial purple 'La France', with the upper petals feathered white and peony purple.

White Petunias mixed with pink ivy-leaved 'Galilee' and again 'La France' is another of my favourite boxes, but there are those who will prefer harder colours such as scarlet Geraniums and magenta 'Vera Dillon', cheek by jowl with purple Petunias. The Petunia is another important window-box plant, whether large-flowered and wavy-edged, free-flowering F1 hybrids, or just the neat and tidy single bedders.

The shady box is more difficult to fill. Having mentioned the tuberous Begonia, let me add the Fuchsia, which enjoys partial shade; the new American rather tender varieties are extremely beautiful if the owner has a gardening friend with a glasshouse who will house them through the winter. Among these, 'Flying Cloud', white with the faintest tint of pink, is superb.

For those who can only entertain the hardy, there is 'Lena', flesh-pink and orchid purple, and the indomitable scarlet and purple 'Mrs Popple', besides the delightful crimson and mauve dwarf 'Tom Thumb'.

For those who have less to spend there are the bright yellow and orange Marigolds, 'Baby Orange' and its successors only 12-15 ins. high, that can be bought as seedlings for a few pence apiece.

Some will prefer the dwarf French varieties, veteran 'Naughty Marietta' or the highly successful 'Yellow Nugget'.

When it comes to Nasturtiums, soft 'Cherry Rose' springs to mind, but 'Golden Orange' and 'Scarlet Gleam' should not be overlooked, nor the neat little bush-maker, 'Baby Salmon'.

Dwarf French Marigolds and Oxford or Cambridge Lobelia planted in block formation make a cheap and telling display.

Maintenance

If the soil was in good order before planting, then there will be no need to feed the plants for a month or so.

No doubt a quick-acting fertilizer will be welcome just before flowering time, particularly in the case of the greedy Petunias and Geraniums. After this, a regular fortnightly dose until the end of the flowering season will be appreciated.

The soil in the box should be thoroughly wetted before the fertilizer is applied and it should be watered in, even if a liquid.

Meanwhile, the gardener should be attentive with the watering-can, never allowing the soil to go dry, but avoiding the soggy. The plants are best allowed to dry out between soakings; dribs and drabs bring thirsty roots to the surface and do more harm than good.

Deadheading should be carried out daily and flowerheads are better picked off before they have altogether faded than left to seed.

26 Fruit

The century-old pears are a great feature of many small gardens in the north of London and particularly in St John's Wood. They and the acacias were planted when the houses were built. I should like to see the pear more freely planted today, provided the garden faces south or south-west and gets plenty of light and sunshine.

When only one fruit tree is to be grown, the gardener should choose a self-fertile variety. The self-sterile will need a second tree as pollinator if it is to set fruit. The nurseryman will give advice as to a suitable cross-pollinating variety, known to do well in your locality.

A standard apple or pear that makes an excellent feature is too large for the average town garden and the dwarf forms grown on suitable stocks should be sought.

Gardeners wishing to grow espaliers trained against wires should consult Long Ashton Research Station, Bristol, where staff are experimenting in growing apples on a wire and bamboo 'palmette' framework. The apple branches are tied at an angle of 45° and the tree built up in tiers, the lateral growth filling the frame.

The family apple-tree carrying three to five different varieties gets much publicity, and the boast that six trees will supply eighteen varieties of fruit is an attractive thought. But it does not always work out that way.

The strongest varieties take over and it is they that fill the baskets, while the more delicate are ousted. However, there is no harm in treating the family tree as an amusing gimmick.

Apples and Pears

Few townsmen grow fruit in a big way, but Mr Basil Dean, the well-known theatrical producer, gathers a considerable crop of fruit year by year from his garden in north London. I give his rewarding orchard list:

Espaliers

Pears	Doyenne de Comice	(1)
	Williams Bon Chrétien	(1)
Apples	Laxton's Superb	(1)
	Beauty of Bath	(1)
	Allington Pippin	(1)
	Cox's Orange	(1)
	Ellison's Orange	(1)
	Worcester Pearmain	(1)
	Sturmer Pippin	(1)

Cordons

Pears	Conference	(2)
Apples	Cox's Orange	(4)
	Worcester Pearmain	(2)
	James Grieve	(1)
	Ribston Pippin	(1)
	Russet	(2)

Standard

Apples	Fortune	(1)

Sub-Standard

Apples	Orleans Reinette	(1)
	American Mother	(1)

Spraying and Pruning Routine

A winter spray of Mortegg is given after Christmas.
Any sign of canker is painted with Medo.
A summer spray against blight is given when the fruitlets fall.

Summer pruning is carried out in late July or August, to discourage growth and enable the sun to get at the fruit.

Winter pruning is carried out in order to keep the trees under control.

The espaliers serve as a background to the roses. In spite of the fact that they deprive the rose-bushes of light and ventilation, they flower well and Mr Dean gets the best of three worlds, pink and white spring blossom, summer and autumn roses, and September fruit.

Pot Fruit-trees

A well-shaped apple- or pear-tree in an 18-in. pot in the courtyard or on the roof is most appealing, both in blossom or fruit. But it will need protection from the frost.

As few townsmen have a cold conservatory, the pot should be sunk in the border, mulched with straw bracken at the end of October, and left under glass until the frosts are over.

The nurseryman can supply suitable pot plants. A good fibrous loam mixed with well-rotted manure sprinkled with bonemeal should be used for planting: over-potting should be avoided, a 12-in. pot will usually be found large enough in the beginning, and firm planting is the rule. Tired soil must be eased away from the roots annually and replaced with fresh compost.

The best time for planting is immediately after leaf-fall. Feeding is helpful once the fruit sets, but should stop immediately the crop shows signs of colouring.

The apple or pear grown from pips off the gardener's plate has an added charm. The seedling that rattled from an apple will generally be inferior to its parent, but there is the rare chance that the growth may raise a desirable new variety.

Figs do well in pots, enjoying the root restriction, and the hardy vines fruit well when root-bound in a barrel sawn in half.

The delicious Black Hamburgh grape should only be attempted in warm southern counties. The great gardener Victoria Sackville-West was a strawberry grape-vine fan and insisted against all comers that the fruit tasted of alpine strawberries rather than pear-drops. Whatever the opinion of the fruit, the grey-pink bunches powdered white are decorative, hanging among the foliage.

Fruiting as well as Flowering Currants are amusing when grown in containers as standards, and the gardener can use his inventiveness in tying, training and controlling soft fruit, the wineberries, loganberries, raspberries and blackberries.

Fans

Peaches and nectarines grow well in the south and in certain favoured gardens in the north and demand a south or south-west wall. They must be given protection against spring frosts, and depend for their success on a good rich soil, a generous supply of lime and efficient drainage.

Plums, usually too big for a small garden, can be trained as a fan on a south wall, and the Morello Cherry is one of the few that really enjoys a north wall.

Now on to one of the best wall plants—the fig. It should be grown against a south wall if fruit is expected, given a loamy soil with a generous mortar rubble content, and its roots, particularly tap-roots, restricted. The roots can be controlled by a brick and concrete barrier.

Strawberries

The strawberry barrel itself has already been dealt with in Chapter 7 (see page 48).

Once the apertures are planted up, the barrel must be placed in a sunny position, four of the largest plants being kept back and installed in the top of the barrel. After this, little attention will be needed, other than the removal of all runners at sight and the application of a generous mulch of manure in March.

The plants can be left undisturbed for three years and it is hoped in these conditions that the birds and the slugs will not make a nuisance of themselves.

'Royal Sovereign' is a difficult variety to beat, but town gardeners should certainly grow one of the little alpine strawberries, among them 'Adolphe Solemacher', as sweet as it is decorative.

27 Vegetables

Cabbages, Brussels, potatoes and others have not been given a place in this book, not because they will not grow in a clean town, but because few town gardeners are interested in their culture. As a rule, they take up too much precious space.

But I am all in favour of introducing ornamental subjects, among them the beautiful variegated Kale. This exotic brassica with curled and fringed foliage in shades of pink, crimson, purple and white is extremely decorative, and I have seen it looking distinguished and dignified planted in an eighteenth-century stone urn. I remember a telling splash of rhubarb in the same garden interplanted with the red-leaf beetroot.

The orange-flowering Runner Bean may or may not fit in with the gardener's colour scheme. Plants can either be grown at the back of a border or grown in the less conventional way, the maypole method. This entails a straight post of about 7 ft. in the centre with strings radiating from the top of the post to ground level. Plants should be kept about 3 ft. apart.

There are always some gardeners who wish to grow their own Lettuce and Tomatoes.

Given a rich moisture-retaining soil, there is no difficulty in growing Lettuce if you sow a suitable variety such as 'Constant Heart', choosing a promising day in March, but seedlings are often a better buy. It is a mistake to try to over-winter crops in difficult areas.

Regularly watered through the dry weather, Lettuce can be kept a delightful bright green, and a line of balcony boxes planted with Lettuce and interplanted with dwarf Marigolds is bright and cheerful.

Perhaps I should add the warning that Lettuce allowed to dry out quickly runs to seed rather than to edible leaf.

Tomatoes must be found a sunny sheltered position if they are to succeed. 'Harbinger' and 'Amateur' are remarkably tolerant if given plenty of room and carefully staked. Side-shoots must be pinched out and the leading shoot dismissed once three trusses have set.

Another warning—keep a watchful look-out for blight, burning affected leaves on sight and spraying with a reputable copper fungicide.

Parsley, already mentioned along with the herbs, is useful in filling any bare patch and a root or two can usually be spared by country friends.

28 Et Ceteras

Greenhouse

The town gardener in his natural desire to hide the greenhouse places it in an unsuitable position—out of the sun.

The ideal situation for the greenhouse is facing west, where it will get the warmth from the evening sun against a cold night. If sheltered from the north and east winds so much the better.

The Shed

A shed for a town garden can sometimes be arranged behind the garage if there is one. It should be, if possible, at least 8 ft. by 6 ft.

The Rubbish Dump

Dustmen who have an objection to removing refuse are not un-common, and it should be pointed out that they have the right to reject anything other than domestic household refuse. Generous tipping is the only answer.

But certain material can be burnt in an incinerator such as the Rapid Standard. The lattice work, although of strong metal, soon deteriorates but a spare body and base can be bought separately for replacements.

The Manhole

Quite a number of gardeners are faced with a manhole and are told by the powers-that-be that they must learn to live with it.

The cover may be of cement or iron (only a little less offensive if of cement) and must on no account be meddled with.

The modern builder seems inordinately proud of the manhole-trademark, and gives it a prominent position on the drive, lawn, terrace or patio, the excuse being that it must be get-at-able.

If set in a concrete area, a giant pot or even a strawberry barrel may be helpful in disguising its presence. Two handles should be fitted to the barrel to facilitate lifting and perhaps two weight-lifting friends invited to do the heaving.

Prostrate shrubs such as *Juniperus Knaphill* or *Cotoneaster horizontalis* are quite effective camouflage. The branches can be staked back or lifted up when 'the man' calls and released without damage when he is gone.

Some gardeners like to dig out the soil round the manhole, and having bricked around it, plant up a screen of vigorous evergreens as camouflage. The operation more often than not merely succeeds in accentuating the presence of an offending structure.

A shallow tray of London Pride and Canary Creeper, House-leek, Sedums, Nasturtiums or Nepeta, is light to carry and more practical. The gardener must have a care that the camouflage is not uglier than the object he seeks to hide.

Moles

Moles are attracted to a lawn where there is an abundance of worms. It may be necessary to reduce the population of these invaders by treating the grass with a reputable wormkiller.

The conventional gardener uses ordinary traps, and some are successful in discouraging the trouble-makers with Topvil Fuses, available from the sundriesman.

The plant *Euphorbia lathyrus*, to be had from the seedsman, is said to keep moles away, but there are divided opinions about the effectiveness of this keep-away spurge.

One of my readers declares that he has solved the menace to his lawn by planting fish-heads and fishbones (raw and cooked) in the mole runs. He digs these into the soil about 1 ft. deep and finds that three fish-heads kept his quarter of an acre free of burrows.

This method should be tried only by those not allergic to the smell of fish.

Hedgehogs

The hedgehog appears to be common in suburbia but on occasion strays into the town. It is a welcome visitor, useful in clearing slugs and snails.

Dogs

There is a Dog and Cat Repellent Cord, impregnated with a scientific formula which is supposed to be effective against dogs, cats, rabbits and other types of animals.

Gardeners have different opinions of the value of this product, and of the various aerosol sprays, as their effect is short-lived.

Stray dogs may dig up plants in a garden but not eat other people's chickens, against which legal action can be taken, and, roughly speaking, cats seem to be allowed to do what they like, however unsocial their behaviour.

I am afraid bitches and lawns do not go together. The damage can be minimized by taking the bitch out for a walk straightaway early in the morning before letting her out in the garden—should the lady escape, you should copiously water the affected area directly afterwards.

Cats

The Dog and Cat Repellent Cord may be tried, but I find the most effective way of protecting favourite plants is to surround them with prickly branches, gorse or what-have-you, as a defence. A mild form of pepper is effective until it rains.

Birds

Morkit is a useful bird repellent spray until the rain washes it away.

It is harmless to humans, animals and even to the birds themselves, but should not be used on edible crops.

The old-fashioned method of the twig and cotton barrage still works, but destroys the appearance of the fairy-like crocus. Scaraweb, a spiderlike fabric of rayon threads, is excellent for protecting fruit buds.

Tools

All gardeners have their favourite tools.

High quality spades and forks are expensive but usually long-lasting and worth the extra money, and a stainless steel spade, if it can be afforded, is a good investment.

There are two points I should like to press home. Light tools are easier to handle than heavy ones and a light well-balanced spade facilitates rhythmic digging that makes light of the work. It is the inclination of the gardener in his salad days to overburden himself with heavy implements.

The second point is the importance of keeping tools clean and sharp.

Earth must be scraped from them with a stout, flat, wedge-ended stick, after which they should be wiped over with an oily rag before they are put away. I am in favour of keeping an impregnated felt block oiler, Lubrafelt, hung in the shed or place where garden implements are kept so that all bladed tools can be wiped over before they are put away. This felt oiler preserves sharp edges, spares hands and minimizes mess. The plastic cap makes a useful scraper.

Tools with a knife-edge should be sent away from time to time to have a knife-edge put on them by a professional grinder.

Within the Law

Never go to law. That is when trouble starts.

The most common litigation concerns the party wall. The title deeds must be carefully examined. Here I give warning—after an expensive legal action, a gardening friend of mine was told that the dilapidated dividing wall between him and his neighbour was 'nobody's legal obligation'. So have a care. Friendly persuasion should always be tried first—at least it is cheap.

Nuisance also begins when trees overhang a neighbouring estate, resulting in unwanted shade and a heavy downfall of tiresome leaves in the neighbouring garden when autumn comes.

This is an encroachment on property and the neighbour has a right to cut the overspreading branches, the fruit or wood removed remaining the property of the owner of the tree, though if he is touchy it may not be wisdom to offer these back to him.

If roots of trees, usually poplars seeking moisture, disturb the foundations of buildings, walls or drainage, the same principle applies, but if damage has been caused the tree owner is liable.

If a neighbour's garden is nothing less than a weed-bed of dandelions with flying seed there is little redress. The Ministry of Agriculture and Fisheries (Weeds Act 1959) is only interested in five proliferating weeds and then only if they are interfering with food production. The listed weeds are: Spear Thistle and Field Thistle, Curled Dock and Broad-leaved Dock, and Ragwort. All unlikely to be found in a town garden.

Bonfires should not be constant and lit only at reasonable times. Manure should not stink and remain stacked close to another person's house or fence for long periods, otherwise nuisances are caused.

ENVOI

I hope this book may lead the reader as through a corridor from house to garden.

INDEX